"*Human + Machine* is a richly detailed guidebook that leaders need to capture the opportunities of AI and the fourth industrial revolution. If we heed Daugherty and Wilson's call to action on reimagining how we work and preparing people for fusion skills, we can ensure a brighter future for all of us."

> —**KLAUS SCHWAB**, founder and Executive Chairman, World Economic Forum; author, *The Fourth Industrial Revolution*

"In the post–Information Age, every sector of the global economy is driven by technology, the source of disruption and new wealth everywhere. For those wishing to participate, you'll need a copy of *Human + Machine*."

> —**MARK ANDERSON**, founder and CEO, Strategic News Service

"In *Human + Machine*, Daugherty and Wilson brilliantly illuminate with real-world examples how companies across every industry are reconceptualizing their businesses and organizations for the age of AI. This is just the beginning of the greatest business transformation in history, with humans and machines working together in ways never before imaginable. As the authors point out, we must invest in training millions of people for the jobs of tomorrow and establish guardrails to ensure that as AI evolves, the benefits accrue to all of humanity. *Human + Machine* is a roadmap to the future—read it if you're serious about understanding the impact of AI and how it is driving growth."

> —**MARC BENIOFF**, Chairman and CEO, Salesforce

"*Human + Machine* is a well-written and well-researched book that addresses the missing middle of AI: how humans and machines can collaborate so as to augment—not replace—human skills. From the manufacturing floor to the back office to the individual, Paul and James offer wonderfully approachable and actionable insight into the changing nature of work."

—**GRADY BOOCH**, Chief Scientist for Software Engineering, IBM Research; IBM Fellow

"*Human + Machine* shines new light on our burning need to reinvent nearly everything about the way we work. Daugherty and Wilson have hands-on experience leading these changes, giving this book an exceptional level of credibility and insight. Have your whole team read it before your competitors do!"

—**ERIK BRYNJOLFSSON**, Director, MIT Initiative on the Digital Economy; coauthor, *The Second Machine Age* and *Machine, Platform, Crowd*

"A must-read for business managers who know AI should be a big part of their job but find the topic intimidating and confusing."

—**MISSY CUMMINGS**, professor, Pratt School of Engineering; Director, Humans and Autonomy Laboratory, Duke University

"We are in an era of digital Darwinism, where technologies are evolving faster than businesses can adapt. Daugherty and Wilson's approaches, the missing middle and MELDS, provide the formula to help you rethink your opportunities, your processes, and your outcomes—with the goal of capturing exponential improvements in record time."

—**CHETAN DUBE**, CEO, IPsoft

"In *Human + Machine*, Daugherty and Wilson give a blueprint for a future in which AI augments our humanity. Packed with examples, instruction, and inspiration, the book is a practical guide to understanding AI—what it means in our lives and how we can make the most of it."

—**ARIANNA HUFFINGTON**, founder and CEO, Thrive Global

"Daugherty and Wilson answer the fundamental question, how do we help our workforce transition into the age of AI? Without question, *Human + Machine* is the handbook you need to move forward."

—**HENNING KAGERMANN**, President, acatech (German Academy of Science and Engineering); former Chairman and CEO, SAP

"The AI revolution has started, so don't fall behind. Read *Human + Machine* cover to cover—and gain the ability to use exponential intelligence and velocity to define and optimize your impact on the world over the coming decade."

—**DAVID KENNY**, Senior Vice President, IBM Watson and IBM Cloud

"*Human + Machine* creates the framework for forward-thinking leaders to develop opportunities within their operating system that optimize both human and machine intelligence; a deeply thought-provoking analysis of how to introduce AI to enhance internal operations and develop a technology-enabled, long-term growth strategy."

—**AARON LEVIE**, CEO, Box

"AI offers great promise to benefit people and society but also presents new challenges and risks. In *Human + Machine*, Daugherty and Wilson have published a crucial perspective on the future of work, illuminating the human-machine relationship in a way that will help us all better understand, discuss, and shape our AI future."

—**TERAH LYONS**, Founding Executive Director, the Partnership on AI; former advisor, White House Office of Science and Technology Policy

"Those of us not trained as technologists must be curious, ongoing learners—then we must apply our learning to job creation in an AI world. *Human + Machine* shows how jobs and tasks can be rethought and redesigned such that people and machines achieve more effective, efficient outcomes together. The book's practical and valuable examples bring the future to life."

—**DOUG MCMILLON**, President and CEO, Walmart

"*Human + Machine* should be assigned reading for anyone struggling with what AI means for their business. It charts a clear path of transformation with human creativity at its heart."

—**VIVIENNE MING**, cofounder and Managing Partner, Socos

"Daugherty and Wilson advance the conversation we need to have about the future of computer and human collaboration with concrete tools such as their 'missing middle' hypothesis and research-based organizational principles. With grounded skill and enthusiasm, the authors have delivered a roadmap that welcomes us to a productive future."

—**SATYA NADELLA**, CEO, Microsoft

"As we prepare for a future where entire industries will be disrupted by machine learning and artificial intelligence, it is imperative to understand how these new technologies work and what impact they can have—positive or negative—on our world. Machine learning and artificial intelligence will impact our world just as profoundly as the invention of the personal computer, the internet, or the smartphone. *Human + Machine* provides a great introduction to prepare for the future. No businessperson can afford to ignore these trends."

—**HADI PARTOVI**, founder and CEO, Code.org

"Daugherty and Wilson provide the insights and actions every organization must take to transform themselves into a thriving digital company."

—**BILL RUH**, Senior Vice President and Chief Digital Officer, GE; CEO, GE Digital

"There is no doubt that AI is transforming business. In *Human + Machine* we are provided a sense of how, where, and most important, what to do about it. The book's sample of 1,500 practitioners provides insights that go way beyond individual anecdotal applications. A must-read for today's manager!"

—**LEN SCHLESINGER**, Baker Foundation Professor, Harvard Business School; former Vice Chairman and Chief Operating Officer, Limited Brands (now L Brands)

"In their insightful book, *Human + Machine*, Daugherty and Wilson paint a picture of humans and machines not as adversaries but as partners. They offer a framework for thinking about the unprecedented implications of this burgeoning relationship and a practical guide to thriving in an era where humans and machines work side by side in service to humanity's advancement."

—**DOV SEIDMAN**, founder and CEO of LRN; author, *HOW: Why HOW We Do Anything Means Everything*

"Advances in AI simultaneously represent great opportunities and even greater disruptions in the times ahead. *Human + Machine* is a very timely and thoughtful work, with examples and strategies to help businesses prepare for AI's impact."

—**DR. VISHAL SIKKA**

"AI will have a profound impact on both society and the economy. Every business leader should get acquainted with the technology and its impact on their market, propositions, and key aspects of the value chain. This is the first comprehensive analysis of the role of AI in business. I consider the book mandatory reading for all leaders who consider innovation essential for their business."

—**JEROEN TAS**, Executive Vice President and Chief Innovation and Strategy Officer, Philips

"Today's fast-moving digital transformation demands relentless re-innovation, continual reeducation, and constant reimagining of what's possible. Your best guide to that future is Daugherty and Wilson's *Human + Machine*."

—**ASHOK VASWANI**, CEO, Barclays UK

"*Human + Machine* stands out as the missing manual that leaders need for AI-driven innovation in today's winner-take-all world."

—**R "RAY" WANG**, Principal Analyst, founder, and Chairman, Constellation Research

HUMAN +
MACHINE

HUMAN +

Reimagining Work in the Age of AI

MACHINE

PAUL R. DAUGHERTY

H. JAMES WILSON

HARVARD BUSINESS REVIEW PRESS

Boston, Massachusetts

Copyright 2018 Accenture Global Solutions Limited

All rights reserved

Printed in the United States of America

10 9 8 7 6 5 4 3 2 1

No part of this publication may be reproduced, stored in or introduced into a retrieval system, or transmitted, in any form, or by any means (electronic, mechanical, photocopying, recording, or otherwise), without the prior permission of the publisher. Requests for permission should be directed to permissions@ hbsp.harvard.edu, or mailed to Permissions, Harvard Business School Publishing, 60 Harvard Way, Boston, Massachusetts 02163.

The web addresses referenced in this book were live and correct at the time of the book's publication but may be subject to change.

Library of Congress Cataloging-in-Publication Data.

Names: Wilson, H. James, author. | Daugherty, Paul R., author.
Title: Human + machine : reimagining work in the age of AI / by H. James Wilson and Paul R. Daugherty.
Description: Boston, Massachusetts : Harvard Business Review Press, [2018]
Identifiers: LCCN 2017044295 | ISBN 9781633693869 (hardcover : alk. paper)
Subjects: LCSH: Technological innovations. | Artificial intelligence. | Business—Data processing.
Classification: LCC T173.8 .W56 2018 | DDC 331.25/6—dc23 LC record available at https://lccn.loc.gov/2017044295

The paper used in this publication meets the requirements of the American National Standard for Permanence of Paper for Publications and Documents in Libraries and Archives Z39.48-1992.

ISBN: 978-1-63369-386-9
eISBN: 978-1-63369-387-6

CONTENTS

PART TWO

The Missing Middle

Reimagining Processes with AI

Those who can imagine anything, can create the impossible.
—Alan Turing

See, the world is full of things more powerful than us. But if you know how to catch a ride, you can go places.
—Neal Stephenson, *Snow Crash*

What's Our Role in the Age of AI?

n one corner of the BMW assembly plant in Dingolfing, Germany, a worker and robot are collaborating to build a transmission. The worker prepares a gear casing, while a lightweight robot arm, sensitive to and aware of its surroundings, picks up a twelve-pound gear. The worker moves on to her next task, while the robot precisely puts the gear inside the casing and turns away to pick up another.

In another part of the plant, where LP's song "Lost on You" hums across the floor, a different lightweight robot arm evenly applies a thick black adhesive to the edge of small car windows. Between applications, a worker walks over to wipe off the glue nozzle, pop in new glass, and carry away the finished windows, as if robot and human are part of a well-choreographed dance.[1]

Thanks to recent advances in artificial intelligence (AI), we are now at the cusp of a major transformation in business. It's a new era in which the fundamental rules by which we run our organizations are being rewritten daily. AI systems are not just automating many processes, making them more efficient; they are now enabling people and machines to work collaboratively in novel ways. In doing so, they are changing the very nature of work, requiring us to manage our operations and employees in dramatically different ways.

For decades, robots have typically been large pieces of machinery, usually sectioned off from human workers, that would perform a dedicated task—unloading a stamping press, for example. That specific task was part of a rigid, fixed chain of work that would generally include humans doing other predefined tasks—for instance, inspecting the stamped metal parts in order to discard defects.

Contrast that traditional assembly line with a factory where robots are much smaller and more flexible, able to work alongside humans. A factory where those robots and other types of machinery are using embedded sensors and sophisticated AI algorithms. Unlike earlier generations of industrial robotics—which were typically bulky, unintelligent, and somewhat dangerous pieces of machinery—these new types of collaborative robots are equipped with the ability to sense their environment, comprehend, act, and learn, thanks to machine-learning software and other related AI technologies. All this then enables the work processes to be self-adapting, with fixed assembly lines giving way to flexible human-machine teams that can be put together on the fly. Now, in order to fulfill customized orders and handle fluctuations in demand, employees can partner with robots to perform new tasks without having to manually overhaul any processes or manufacturing steps. Those changes are baked into the system and are performed automatically.

The advances are not just in manufacturing. AI systems are being integrated across all departments, everything from sales and marketing to customer service to product R&D.

Take, for instance, a designer at Autodesk who decides to build a drone. Instead of modifying preexisting concepts and adjusting for various constraints like weight and propulsion, she inputs these parameters into the company's AI-enabled software. The software's genetic algorithm produces a vast and dizzying array of new designs that no one has ever seen. Some are more bizarre than others, but all fit the initial constraints. The designer chooses one that will distinguish her drone from the rest and further tweaks the design to fit her aesthetic and engineering goals.

From the Mechanistic to the Organic

The potential power of AI to transform businesses is unprecedented, and yet there is an urgent and growing challenge. Companies are now reaching a crossroad in their use of AI, which we define *as systems that extend human capability by sensing, comprehending, acting, and learning.* As businesses deploy such systems—spanning from machine learning to computer vision to deep learning—some firms will continue to see modest productivity gains over the short run, but those results will eventually stall out. Other companies will be able to attain breakthrough improvements in performance, often by developing game-changing innovations. What accounts for the difference?

It has to do with understanding the true nature of AI's impact. In the past, executives focused on using machines to automate specific workflow processes. Traditionally, these processes were linear, stepwise, sequential, standardized, repeatable, and measurable, and over the years they've been optimized through various time-and-motion analyses (think of those manufacturing assembly lines). But performance gains from that approach have recently been leveling off, as companies wring the last bits of efficiencies from mechanistic automation.

Now, to continue exploiting the full potential of AI technologies, many leading companies have begun to embrace a new view of business processes as more fluid and adaptive. In essence, they are moving beyond rigid assembly lines toward the idea of organic teams that partner humans with advanced AI systems. This collaboration between workers and smart machines is leading to the reinvention of many traditional processes. As BMW and Mercedes-Benz have experienced, rigid assembly lines are giving way to flexible teams of employees working closely alongside robots. Moreover, these novel types of teams can continuously adapt on the fly to new data and market conditions. They are enabling companies to actually *reimagine* various work processes.

The Third Wave

The key to understanding AI's current and future impact is its transformation of *business processes*.

A widespread misconception is that AI systems, including advanced robotics and digital bots, will gradually replace humans in one industry after another. Self-driving vehicles, for example, will one day replace taxi, delivery, and truck drivers. That may be true for certain jobs, but what we've found in our research is that, although AI can be deployed to automate certain functions, the technology's greater power is in comple-menting and *augmenting* human capabilities. In claims pro-cessing, for example, AI isn't replacing the need for humans; instead, it's doing the tedious grunt work, collecting data and doing a preliminary analysis, freeing human claims processors to focus on resolving complex cases. In essence, machines are doing what they do best: performing repetitive tasks, analyz-ing huge data sets, and handling routine cases. And humans are doing what they do best: resolving ambiguous information, exercising judgment in difficult cases, and dealing with dissatis-fied customers. This kind of emerging symbiosis between man and machine is unlocking what we have called *the third wave of business transformation*.

To see how we got here, it helps to understand some historical context. The first wave of business transformation involved *standardized* processes. This era was ushered in by Henry Ford, who deconstructed the manufacture of automobiles so that they could be made on an assembly line. Each of those steps in that overall process could then be measured, optimized, and stan-dardized to achieve considerable gains in efficiencies.

The second wave consisted of *automated* processes. This era emerged in the 1970s and peaked in the 1990s with the business process reengineering (BPR) movement, thanks to advances in information technology (IT): desktop computers, large data-bases, and software that automated various back-office tasks. Among other companies, retailers like Walmart rode this wave to become worldwide powerhouses. Other firms were able to reinvent themselves. UPS, for example, transformed itself from a package-delivery service to a global logistics company.

Now, the third wave involves *adaptive* processes. This third era, which builds on the previous two, will be more dramatic than the earlier revolutions enabled by assembly lines and digital computers, and will usher in entirely new, innovative ways of doing business. As we will see throughout this book, the leading firms in many industries are now reimagining their processes to be more flexible, faster, and adaptable to the behaviors, preferences, and needs of their workers at a given moment. This adaptive capability is being driven by real-time data rather than by an a priori sequence of steps. The paradox is that although these processes are not standardized or routine, they can repeatedly deliver better outcomes. In fact, leading organizations have been able to bring to market individualized products and services (as opposed to the mass-produced goods of the past), as well as deliver profitable outcomes.

Think Like Waze

To help illustrate the profound difference between the old process thinking and the new, consider the history of GPS navigation. The first online maps were largely just a digital version of their paper counterparts. But soon, GPS navigation devices changed how we used maps, giving us directions after entering a destination. Even that, though, was still a fairly static process. Now, mobile map apps like Waze are taking advantage of real-time user data—about drivers' locations and speeds as well as crowdsourced information about traffic jams, accidents, and other obstructions to create the perfect map in real time. All that data enables the system to update directions en route so that, if necessary, it can reroute drivers midcourse to minimize any possible delays. Whereas the old approach with GPS simply digitized a static paper-map route, Waze has combined AI algorithms and real-time data to create living, dynamic, optimized maps that can get people to their destinations as quickly as possible. Business approaches that use AI merely for automating existing static processes are like the early GPS navigation devices, whereas the current era of symbiotic collaborations between humans and machines are like Waze in that those traditional processes are being completely reimagined.

Filling the "Missing Middle"

Unfortunately, popular culture has long promoted a man-versus-machine view—think of movies such as *2001: A Space Odyssey* and the *Terminator* series. The idea of intelligent machines as a potential threat to mankind has a long history and has resulted in many executives adopting a somewhat similar perspective, thinking exclusively of machines as threatening to replace humans. But that view is not only woefully misguided; it's also perniciously shortsighted.

The simple truth is that machines are not taking over the world, nor are they obviating the need for humans in the workplace. In this current era of business process transformation, AI systems are not wholesale replacing us; rather, they are amplifying our skills and collaborating with us to achieve productivity gains that have previously not been possible.

As you shall see in this book, the third wave has created a huge, dynamic, and diverse space in which humans and machines collaborate to attain orders-of-magnitude increases in business performance. We call this the "missing middle"—"missing" because almost no one talks about it, and only a small fraction of companies are working to fill this crucial gap (see figure I-1).

FIGURE I-1

The missing middle

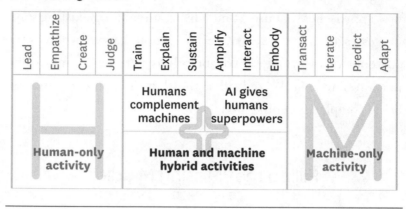

Lead	Empathize	Create	Judge	Train	Explain	Sustain	Amplify	Interact	Embody	Transact	Iterate	Predict	Adapt
				Humans complement machines			AI gives humans superpowers						
Human-only activity				**Human and machine hybrid activities**						**Machine-only activity**			

In the missing middle, humans work with smart machines to exploit what each party does best. Humans, for example, are needed to develop, train, and manage various AI applications. In doing so, they are *enabling* those systems to function as true collaborative partners. For their part, machines in the missing middle are helping people to punch above their weight, providing them with superhuman capabilities, such as the ability to process and analyze copious amounts of data from myriad sources in real time. Machines are *augmenting* human capabilities.

In the missing middle, humans and machines aren't adversaries, fighting for each other's jobs. Instead, they are symbiotic partners, each pushing the other to higher levels of performance. Moreover, in the missing middle, companies can reimagine their business processes to take advantage of collaborative teams of humans working alongside machines. It's not just digital companies that are exploiting the missing middle. Rio Tinto, the global mining conglomerate, is a case in point. The company is using AI to manage its vast fleet of machinery—autonomous drills, excavators, earth movers, and so on—from a central control facility. This has freed human operators from working in dangerous mining conditions and also enabled Rio Tinto's team of data analysts to analyze information from sensors on the remote equipment to uncover valuable insights for helping the firm manage its fleet more efficiently and safely.[2]

Separating Winners from Losers— and What's in This Book

As we mentioned earlier, in the current era of adaptive processes, the fundamental rules by which organizations are run are being rewritten daily. As leaders and managers in all kinds of enterprises begin to reimagine their business processes and rethink the basic relationship between employees and machines, they must understand those rules and execute on them. That's why we wrote this book: to give people who are thinking about their organization, their team, or their career the knowledge they need that will separate winners from losers in the new age of AI.

In part one, we show and explain the current state of AI in companies. We begin on the shop floor, and in subsequent chapters, illustrate how organizations are currently deploying AI in different functions—back office, R&D, marketing, and sales. A key lesson here is that companies can't expect to benefit from human-machine collaborations without first laying the proper groundwork. Again, those companies that are using machines merely to replace humans will eventually stall, whereas those that think of innovative ways for machines to augment humans will become the leaders of their industries.

Chapter 1 describes how human-machine teams are transforming the factory floor, not just at BMW and Mercedes-Benz but also at many other large manufacturers. General Electric, for example, has been building "digital twins" of its deployed products, like the turbine blades on a jet engine. The company bases these virtual models on the current conditions of real machinery, enabling it to improve operations as well as predict breakdowns before they occur, thus fundamentally changing how it maintains commercial equipment.

The focus is back-office operations in chapter 2. Here, AI technology can help filter and analyze streams of information from a variety of sources and enable the automation of tedious, repetitive tasks as well as the augmentation of human skills and expertise. At a Canadian insurance and financial service provider, for example, an AI system processes unstructured financial data from news articles, reports, and emails to make specific recommendations, and the system can be trained to extract insights tailored to an individual analyst's preferences.

Chapter 3 describes how companies are using AI in research and development. In each major step of the R&D process—observation, hypothesis generation, experiment design, and results analysis—AI technologies can lead to increased efficiencies and markedly improved outcomes. At GNS Healthcare, sophisticated machine-learning software finds patterns in patient medical health records and then automatically churns out hypotheses straight from that data. The system took just three months to recreate the results of a two-year study investigating adverse reactions between drug combinations in seniors on Medicare.

We turn to the marketing and sales function and describe how the impact of AI has been just as great—if not more so—as in other functions in chapter 4. Machine-learning technologies like Amazon's Alexa, Apple's Siri, and Microsoft's Cortana are increasingly becoming the digital embodiment of those companies' well-known brands. In other words, AI has become the brand.

In part two, we explore the "missing middle" and provide an executive guide for overhauling and "reimagining" the traditional notions of work. To exploit the full power of AI, companies must fill that gap by considering new employee roles, by establishing novel types of working relationships between humans and machines, by changing traditional concepts of management, and by overhauling their very concept of work itself.

Chapter 5 describes how machine learning, when integrated into processes, will lead to a variety of brand-new jobs. Specifically, employees will be needed to design and train algorithms, to explain the algorithms used, and to do so in a way that sustains the algorithms within a process. One such new role is that of *machine relations managers*, who will be similar to human resources managers except they will oversee AI systems instead of human workers. They will be responsible for regularly conducting performance reviews of a company's AI systems. They will promote those systems that perform well, replicating variants and deploying them to other parts of the organization. Those systems with poor performance will be demoted and possibly decommissioned.

In chapter 6, we describe how people are achieving huge performance boosts by working with AI technologies that dramatically improve their human capabilities; they amplify, interact, and embody new human potential. (In a sense, this chapter is the flip side of chapter 5, in which we discussed how humans are helping machines to extend and amplify their capabilities.) These new types of human-machine relationships are helping people to "punch above their weight" by offloading tedious tasks and by enabling them to perform their work faster and more effectively through the expert guidance, advice, and support from AI systems.

Chapter 7 takes a hard look at managerial challenges introduced by AI that require different, new responses from management and leadership. A huge question here is, what steps must management take to facilitate reimagining processes? Specifically, management must support five crucial activities, including an emphasis on trial-and-error *experimentation,* building a *data supply chain* for AI, and others.

Finally, we explore the future of work itself in chapter 8. Specifically, as human-machine collaborations become increasingly prevalent, companies will need to hire for and develop eight new "fusion skills": *intelligent interrogation* (knowing how best to ask an AI agent questions, across levels of abstraction, to get the insights you need), *bot-based empowerment* (collaborating with intelligent agents to punch above your weight at work), *reciprocal apprenticing* (teaching AI agents new skills while also undergoing on-the-job training to work well within AI-enhanced processes), *holistic melding* (developing mental models of AI agents that improve collaborative outcomes), *rehumanizing time* (reimagining business processes to amplify the time available for distinctly human tasks and learning), *responsible normalizing* (shaping the purpose and perception of human-machine collaborations as it relates to individuals, businesses, and society), *judgment integration* (choosing a course of action amid machine uncertainty), and *relentless reimagining* (thinking of novel ways to overhaul work, processes, and business models to obtain exponential increases in improvement).

Five Crucial Principles

In our research, we have found that the leading companies in various industries—9 percent of our surveyed sample of more than fifteen hundred practitioners—are already riding the third wave. They have maximized automation and are now developing the next generation of processes and skills to capitalize on human-machine collaborations. They are thinking as Waze does, re-imagining processes as living and adaptive by using human and crowd inputs and real-time data. They are moving beyond the traditional thinking of simply digitalizing the old static maps.

How have these leading firms been accomplishing that? In our work, we found that they have succeeded by adopting five crucial principles having to do with their organizational mindset, experimentation, leadership, data, and skills (MELDS).

- *Mindset: assuming a radically different approach toward business by reimagining work around the missing middle, wherein people improve AI and, in turn, smart machines give humans superpowers.* Previously, the focus was on using machines to automate specific steps in a given work flow. Now, the potential collaboration between humans and machines is leading to the reinvention of many traditional processes. Rigid assembly lines are giving way to flexible teams of augmented humans and smart machines. Moreover, these teams are continuously adapting on the fly to new data and to different human contributions. They are truly organic, with the associated work processes akin to living and breathing organisms. We foresee that AI technologies will be critical in helping companies bring work closer to the markets they serve, improving responsiveness to consumer demand. To achieve that, however, executives must embrace a distinctive, action-oriented mindset to reimagine their operations, as we will discuss throughout the book. That said, executives must also understand that they need to lay a foundation first instead of rushing to fill the missing middle. Specifically, they initially should focus on developing the full potential of their employees by applying automation to routine work; then they can proceed to concentrate on human-machine collaborations.

- *Experimentation: actively observing for spots in processes to test AI and to learn and scale a reimagined process from the perspective of the missing middle.* The age of standard business processes is coming to an end, and companies will no longer be able to rely on a strategy of replicating best-in-class practices from leading firms. And this is why experimentation is crucial. Executives must continually conduct tests to derive business processes that will work best for their unique set of conditions. A large part of that effort will require trial and error to determine what work should be done by humans, and what work would best be done by a collaboration between humans and machine (the missing middle).

- *Leadership: making a commitment to the responsible use of AI from the start.* Executives must always consider the ethical, moral, and legal implications of the AI technologies they deploy, and the systems must generate explainable results, promote algorithmic accountability, and eliminate biases. Firms also need to pay close attention to ensure that the employees working with AI systems don't lose a sense of agency and that those individuals develop a heightened sense of empowerment in decision making. In addition, companies must provide the employee training and retraining required so that people will be prepared and ready to assume any new roles in the missing middle. In fact, investing in people must be a core part of any company's AI strategy.

- *Data: building a data "supply chain" to fuel intelligent systems*. AI requires extensive amounts of data, both in volume and variety. This includes "exhaust data"—data created as a byproduct of another process (for example, cookies from customer web browsing). Accumulating and preparing such information for use is one of the biggest challenges for organizations that deploy AI systems. Moreover, an organization's data should be able to flow freely, unencumbered by departmental silos. A company can then take full advantage of that information by applying it and other data to support, sustain, and improve AI and human performance in the missing middle.

- *Skills: actively developing the eight "fusion skills" necessary for reimagining processes in the missing middle*. The growing power of AI is fundamentally transforming the human-machine relationship. In the second wave, machines were generally being used to replace humans—think of how automation has decimated the ranks of factory workers, administrative assistants, bookkeepers, bank tellers, travel agents, and so on. But humans are needed now more than ever in the third wave. Humans are taking center stage in this current era of business process improvement. Specifically, the era of adaptive processes requires humans in the loop, not only to design, develop, and train AI systems, but also to collaborate with them to fill the missing middle and achieve step-level increases in performance.

As you will see, the MELDS framework guides nearly all of the practical aspects of the book, and we will return to it many times throughout. In particular, chapter 7 will focus intently on "MELD," while chapter 8 will dive deeply into the "S".

———————

The AI revolution is not coming; it is already here, and it is about reimagining your processes, across all functions of the company, to get the most benefit from this technology's power to augment human capability. This book is your road map for understanding and navigating the new landscape. Let's get started.

PART ONE

Imagining a Future of Humans + Machines . . . Today

1

The Self-Aware Factory Floor

AI in Production, Supply Chain, and Distribution

For centuries, factories have been the paragon of automation. And the people who work in factories, as a result, have often been measured by the standards of machines. So it's no surprise that the relationship between people and machines in industry has been fraught, with human workers feeling as if they've been dealt a losing hand. There's ample reason for that feeling. Since 2000, the United States has lost five million manufacturing jobs, roughly half of that through efficiency gains and automation.[1]

But things aren't as clear cut as they might first seem. As we discussed in the previous chapter, the second wave of business transformation was all about *automating existing processes*, and it was during this era that many humans were replaced by machines. In contrast, the third wave relies on *adaptive* processes that are reimagined from scratch, and the goal here is humans + machines. In this current era, thanks to AI, factories are acquiring a little more humanity: jobs on manufacturing lines, for instance, have changed in nature and are increasing in number. And it's not just manufacturing. AI is boosting the value of engineers and managers, too. The emergence of AI is also creating brand-new roles and new opportunities for people up and down the industrial value chain.

In this era of reimagining processes with AI, the great irony is that some of the most-automated environments—the factory and other industrial settings—are experiencing a renaissance of human labor. From the assembly-line worker and maintenance specialist to robot engineer and operations manager, AI is rejiggering the concept of what it means to work in an industrial setting. In many cases, AI is freeing up time, creativity, and human capital, essentially letting people work more like humans and less like robots. One implication of the fact that people can work differently and better with the help of AI is that companies are gaining efficiencies and saving money. But perhaps more importantly in the long term is that companies are also starting to rethink their business processes. And as they do, they uncover the need for new kinds of jobs for people, and wholly new ways of doing business, which is our focus in part two of this book.

But let's not get ahead of ourselves. This is a complex journey. (For some historical perspective, see the sidebar "A Brief History of AI" at the end of this chapter.) Before we rewrite business processes, job descriptions, and business models, we need to answer these questions: what tasks do humans do best, and what do machines do best? There are jobs and tasks that will continue to shift to robots based on their comparative advantages in handling repetition and data processing power. But as we'll see, the transfer of jobs is not simply one way. In this chapter, we survey a number of companies that have already answered the human-machine question for manufacturing, maintenance, warehouses, and agriculture. These early movers have put people and AI-enhanced machines into play, in the roles that they're best suited to, and they are reaping the benefits.

The Arm That Learns

The third shift in a Tokyo factory is showtime for an emerging class of robotic arms that can learn new tricks overnight. Coupled with a camera and machine-learning software, these hinged and swiveling appendages can, on their own, figure out the most efficient ways to pick up parts and pieces and set them down somewhere else. No explicit programming is necessary.[2]

Robotic arms are used in factories to apply hot glue to widgets, to install windshields, and to smooth jagged metal edges, among other tasks. But, traditionally, engineers have preprogrammed them. Then, when robots' jobs change, engineers must reprogram them. In contrast, the new robotic arms, developed by Fanuc in partnership with software-maker Preferred Networks (both based in Japan), adapt on their own. They do it with an AI technique called deep reinforcement learning, in which the robot is given a picture of the successful outcome and then uses trial and error to figure out its own solution.

According to Shohei Hido, chief research officer at Preferred Networks, the arms take eight hours to become at least 90 percent accurate for this kind of task. This is virtually the same time and accuracy of an expert programming it, but because the arm is now autodidactic, the human expert is now freed to do other more complex tasks, especially those that require human judgment. What's more, once one robot learns a task, it can share its knowledge with other robots in the network. This means that eight arms working together for one hour can learn as much as one working on a problem for eight hours. Hido, who calls this process "distributed learning," says, "You can imagine hundreds of factory robots sharing information."[3]

Now, imagine people working alongside these robots. Mechanical arms are great for highly repetitive tasks and heavy lifting, but in any factory, there will always be a subset of tasks that are just too complex to hand off to a robot—tasks like positioning numerous small wires or handling awkward or dynamic objects. A human is still needed in the loop.

So how do robot arms and humans work together? Historically, not so well. Robots, with their fast, decisive movements have been helpful and efficient, but also dangerous to people. They've often been cordoned off behind protective barriers. But that standard segregation is beginning to change. So-called collaborative robots from companies like Rethink Robotics, founded by robotics and AI pioneer Rodney Brooks, come equipped with sensors that allow them to recognize a range of objects and avoid knocking people around. When robots aren't so clumsy, they can work well with people. Factories that use Rethink Robotics products often divide the work between the robot and the human worker, working side by side, performing tasks best suited to their abilities. (For further examples of embodied AI, see the sidebar "AI in the Factory.")

AI in the Factory

For a century, factory floors have been at the leading edge in robotic automation. From conveyor belts to robotic arms to AI-infused operations systems, the factory is getting smarter every day.

- Hitachi is using AI to analyze big data and workers' routines to inform its robots, which deliver instructions to employees to meet real-time fluctuating demand and on-site kaizen objectives. In a pilot, the company observed an 8 percent productivity improvement in logistics tasks.[a]

- At Siemens, armies of spider-styled 3-D printed robots use AI to communicate and collaborate to build things in the company's Princeton, New Jersey, lab. Each bot is equipped with vision sensors and laser scanners. In aggregate, they join forces to manufacture on the go.[b]

- At Inertia Switch, robotic intelligence and sensor fusion enable robot-human collaboration. The manufacturing firm uses Universal Robotics' robots, which can learn tasks on the go and can flexibly move between tasks, making them handy helpers to humans on the factory floor.[c]

a. Dave Gershgorn, "Hitachi Hires Artificially Intelligent Bosses for Their Warehouses," *Popular Science*, September 8, 2015, www.popsci.com/hitachi-hires-artificial-intelligence-bosses-for-their-warehouses.

b. Mike Murphy, "Siemens is building a swarm of robot spiders to 3D-print objects together," *Quartz*, April 29, 2016, https://qz.com/672708/siemens-is-building-a-swarm-of-robot-spiders-to-3d-print-objects-together/.

c. Robotiq, "Inertia Switch Case Study – Robotiq 2-Finger Adaptive Gripper – ROBOTIQ," YouTube video, 1:32 minutes, posted July 28, 2014, https://www.youtube.com/watch?v=iJftrfiGyfs.

Kindler, Gentler Robots

During the second AI "winter," Rodney Brooks challenged one of the fundamental ideas that had driven previous AI research—namely, the reliance on predetermined symbols and relationships between symbols to help computers make sense of the world (see the sidebar "Two AI Winters"). He claimed a much more robust approach: instead of cataloging the world in advance and representing it with symbols, why not survey it with sensors instead? "The world is its own best model," he wrote in a famous 1990 paper called "Elephants Don't Play Chess." (Brooks would later found iRobot, maker of the robotic vacuum Roomba, as well as Rethink Robotics. To date, iRobot has deployed the largest fleet of autonomous robots in the world: between 2002 and 2013, more than 10 million were sold.[4])

Now, Brooks's AI philosophy is alive and well in both research and industry. Rethink Robotics, in particular, demonstrates the power of an arm equipped with embedded sensors and algorithms for motion control that allow it to "feel" its way and adjust as it goes. The arm features elastic actuators and back-drivable joints, which means it can flex on contact to absorb energy. Consequently, even if it does knock into something (or someone), it wouldn't have nearly the force of a traditional robotic arm.

What's possible when robot arms can learn on their own, as with Fanuc's products? Or when an arm operates in a kinder, gentler way, as with Rethink's products?

On the assembly line, workers can collaborate with a self-aware robot arm. Say a worker is putting together a car and needs to put

Two AI Winters

The path to human-machine collaboration—a hallmark of the third wave of process improvement—was far from smooth. AI was initially greeted with considerable enthusiasm, only to be followed by results that didn't live up to the initial hype, and then more progress, leading to a second wave of hype then disappointment. Those down periods have become known as AI's two "winters."

The field of AI began in the 1950s, and during the decades that followed any research progress came only in fits and starts. By the 1970s, funding had dissipated so much that the era became known as the first AI winter. Then, during a few years in the 1980s, some researchers made progress in so-called expert systems—computer systems loaded with code that allowed a machine to perform a kind of rudimentary reasoning using "if-then" rules rather than following a strict, predetermined algorithm. But the desktop computer revolution was under way, and attention was diverted toward personal computers as they became increasingly affordable and practical for the average person. Again, money for AI dried up, and the second AI winter descended. It wasn't until the 2000s that AI began to draw major investment again.

an interior panel on one of its doors. The robot can lift the panel and position it into place, while the worker performs fine adjustments and fastening without fear that a clunky machine will clock him in the head. AI helps both robots and people play to their strengths, and in the process, the assembly line changes shape.

One way that assembly lines can be reconfigured is through AI itself. Engineers at the Fraunhofer Institute of Material Flow and Logistics (IML) have been testing embedded sensors to create self-adapting assembly lines in car plants. Essentially, the line itself can modify the steps in its process to fit the demands of various features and add-ons for highly customizable cars. Thus, instead of engineers designing an assembly line to make one kind of car at a time, these lines can adapt as needed. What's more, says Andreas Nettsträter, who coordinates strategic initiatives at IML, "If one station has a failure or is broken down, the others could also do what should have been done in this assembly station."[5]

This means that assembly-line workers are doing tasks that are less robotic (saving those tasks for the robot) and more nuanced, while process engineers don't need to reconfigure the line every time there's a change in demand or breakdown of a machine. They can spend their time working on more creative tasks to eke out further efficiencies, for instance.

Follow the Data

What starts with smart arms can extend to an entire factory line and beyond: AI-enabled processes throughout manufacturing and industrial environments are freeing up human potential in a variety of contexts. Maintenance work, for instance, has been forever upended by AI. Sophisticated AI systems predict machine breakdowns *before* they occur, which means that maintenance workers can spend less time running routine checks and diagnostics and more time fixing a company's assets. (For other applications, see the sidebars "AI for Faster Machine Onboarding" and "AI in the Field—Unmanned Vehicles.")

AI for Faster Machine Onboarding

Sight Machine, a startup in San Francisco, uses machine-learning analytics to enable its customers to reduce down-time when adding new machines to a factory floor. In one case, the technology was able to reduce a customer's down-time, usually inherent in breaking in new robotic systems, by 50 percent. In addition, the net gain was a 25 percent increase in performance when all the assets were up and running. Furthermore, not only does the technology help improve factory efficiency, but it also allows engineers and maintenance workers to spend more time tackling other, higher-value tasks.[a]

a. "Jump Capital, GE Ventures, and Two Roads Join $13.5 Million Series B Investment in Sight Machine," Sight Machine, March 22, 2016, http://sightmachine .com/resources/analytics-news-and-press/jump-capital-ge-ventures-and-two -roads-join-13-5-million-series-b-investment-in-sight-machine/.

General Electric, for example, keeps track of its products in the field using its AI-enabled system called Predix. The system relies on a "digital twin" concept in which all assets of a factory and beyond—from bolt to conveyor belt to turbine blade—are monitored and modeled on a computer. Predix collects and manages a lot of data, and it can be put to use to reimagine business processes in three fundamental ways:

- *Reimagined maintenance*. GE keeps stats from the point of installation from a large number of customers and uses machine-learning technology to predict when certain parts might fail based on their current conditions.

AI in the Field—Unmanned Vehicles

Acting as an extra pair of eyes in the sky or under the sea, drones, powered by AI, can keep human workers out of harm's way by allowing teams to remotely explore potentially dangerous terrain.

- Fortescue Metals Group, which operates the Cloudbreak iron ore mine, uses drones there to gather spatial information. Its fleet of flying robots has significantly reduced the safety risk to operators in high-risk areas.[a]

- At BHP Billiton Ltd., unmanned aerial vehicles equipped with infrared sensors and telescopic zoom can flag problems with safety beams and roads under construction. They also check blast zones to make sure they're clear of people before detonation.[b]

- Boeing's "Echo Voyager" is an unmanned deep-sea robot that inspects underwater infrastructures, takes water samples, creates maps of the ocean floor, and aids in oil and gas exploration.[c]

a. Allie Coyne, "Fortescue deploys survey drones at Cloudbreak mine," *IT News*, August 31, 2015, https://www.itnews.com.au/news/fortescue-deploys -survey-drones-at-cloudbreak-mine-408550.

b. Rhiannon Hoyle, "Drones, Robots Offer Vision of Mining's Future," *Wall Street Journal*, July 28, 2016, http://www.wsj.com/articles/drones-robots -offer-vision-of-minings-future-1469757666.

c. "Boeing's Monstrous Underwater Robot Can Wander the Ocean for 6 Months," *Wired*, March 21, 2016, https://www.wired.com/2016/03/boeings -monstrous-underwater-robot-can-wander-ocean-6-months/.

Previously, maintenance professionals would have a fixed schedule for checking or replacing certain parts— something like switching out a car's spark plugs every seventy-five thousand miles; checks and replacements can now happen on an as-needed basis. AI-enhanced prediction saves money and time, and it has the potential to keep maintenance workers more engaged in their jobs.[6]

- *Reimagined product development.* More data leads to improved R&D. GE is now attaching sensors to some of the hottest parts of turbines so that it can monitor physical changes. The sensors literally burn off at operating temperatures, but by that time, data from the turbine's cold-to-hot transition has been collected. This information can then help engineers better understand the thermodynamics of the materials used in the turbines and potentially improve that product's operating conditions. Engineers, thanks to AI, now have more data than ever to understand the operations of their systems.[7]

- *Reimagined operations.* The field data collected also enables GE to build digital twins of its deployed products, like its jet engines. Engineers can then test virtual flights in which the plane experiences cold, heat, dust, rain, and even a flock of birds.[8] The company is also monitoring ten thousand wind turbines, and their digital twins are helping the turbines to adapt in real time. One valuable insight from an analysis of that data is that, depending on the direction of the wind, it might be best to have the leading turbine run slower than engineers might expect. When the front turbine absorbs less energy, the ones behind it can operate at close to their optimal levels, increasing energy generation overall. This application shows that digital twin technology can be applied beyond a single product to holistically optimize an entire wind farm's activity. According to GE, digital twins could increase wind-farm output by 20 percent and provide $100 million of value over the lifetime of a 100-megawatt wind farm.[9]

All three of these uses of Predix are freeing up human workers to do less routine work and more engaging work. The maintenance worker gets to spend more time on tricky fixes and less time on routine monitoring. The engineer has more data with which to see system successes and failures, which can lead to more creative solutions down the line. And finally, the digital twin models are providing an experimental space that's vastly larger than that in which most engineers play. These models allow engineers to be more creative in the questions they ask and allow for the emergence of previously hidden inefficiencies—with the potential for significant savings of time and money.

The Warehouse That's Packed

Today, it's not uncommon to walk into a modern warehouse or distribution center and see robots rolling along the floor. (For a small sampling of these smarter supply chain and warehouse bots, see the sidebar "AI in Warehouse and Logistics.")

AI in Warehouse and Logistics

Artificial intelligence is taking on the task of warehouse navigation and inventory and changing the way people think about warehouse design.

- When Amazon acquired Kiva Robots in 2012, it signaled that the mobile bots zipping around Amazon's warehouses were a key to their fulfillment advantage. Not only do the robots help lift and stack plastic bins filled with different products, they also do the legwork of autonomously transporting items around the facility to human "pickers," who then select the right products to fulfill different orders. Thanks to such increased efficiencies, the company has been able to offer same-day shipping for customers.[a]

- L'Oreal uses radio-frequency identification (RFID) technology and machine learning to help prevent forklift accidents in the company's warehouse in Italy. The tracking system warns forklift operators and pedestrians about other nearby vehicles, cutting down on collisions.[b]

a. Nick Wingfield, "As Amazon Pushes Forward with Robots, Workers Find New Roles," *New York Times*, September 10, 2017, https://www.nytimes.com/2017/09/10/technology/amazon-robots-workers.html.

b. Claire Swedberg, "L'Oréal Italia Prevents Warehouse Collisions via RTLS," *RFID Journal*, August 18, 2014, http://www.rfidjournal.com/articles/view?12083/2.

These robots are often sophisticated enough to see where they're going and understand what they're doing. But they have their limitations. Say a case of Cheerios is damaged, making it bulkier on one side. Most robots can't adapt. They'd need to skip it and move along to the next case. But robots from a company called Symbotic have the advantage of machine vision algorithms that allow them to assess an oddly shaped package and pick it up anyway. Even better, the robots can quickly measure shelf space to confirm that a box will fit. If it won't, the robot alerts a central control system, which automatically redirects that box to a shelf where it will fit. The bots zip around the warehouse floor at twenty-five miles per hour, carrying, sensing, and adapting as they go.

The difference between a traditional warehouse and one with Symbotic's robots is stark. Usually, trucks unload pallets of products at the dock; there's an area where pallets are stored until people can unpack them, and conveyor belts move cases of goods to various parts of the warehouse. But because the Symbotic robots immediately remove products from pallets and put them on shelves, there's no need to reserve space for storing pallets. And there's no need for conveyor belts either. Thus, a Symbotic-equipped warehouse can reclaim space for shelves. The ramifications are significant: in the best-case scenarios, either a warehouse can store twice as many goods as before, says Joe Caracappa, Symbotic vice president of business development, or it can operate in an area about half the size. Moreover, smaller warehouses can more easily fit into existing neighborhoods, and perishable items can be stored closer to their point of sale.

Because the only human interaction with the goods stored at a warehouse is when they're loaded on and off the trucks, we must ask the question: What happens to the human workers at the warehouse? Caracappa says Symbotic currently retrains many of them. Those who performed maintenance on conveyor belts, for instance, are trained to fix robots. And there are new roles, too. Caracappa says system operators monitor the entire flow of robots. "Those roles are typically not in the warehouse before automation comes in," he explains, "but we'll hire them locally and the client will be part of the process."[10] (In part two of this book, we will explore these new types of jobs in depth when we discuss the missing middle in detail.)

Supply Chains That Think

Smarter warehouses are just the beginning. AI technologies are now enabling entire supply chains to become increasingly intelligent, similar to the kinds of advances they've enabled on the factory floor. Of course, companies want to minimize any upstream disruptions to their supply chains, which can come from a number of sources—manufacturing quality problems at a supplier, political instability of a region, labor strikes, adverse weather events, and so on. To that end, AI can help collect and analyze data about suppliers, provide a better understanding of the variables in a supply chain, anticipate future scenarios, and so on. And firms also want to minimize downstream uncertainties. Here, AI can enable companies to optimize their demand planning, forecast more accurately, and better control their inventories. The result is more-agile supply chains capable of anticipating and dealing with the ups and downs of dynamic business conditions.

Consider just one part of the process: demand planning. Getting demand planning right is a pain point for many companies, but the use of neural networks, machine-learning algorithms, and other AI technologies can help lessen that pain. A leading health-food company, for example, leveraged machine-learning capabilities to analyze its demand variations and trends during promotions. The analysis led to a reliable, detailed model that could highlight the expected results from a trade promotion. The gains included a 20 percent reduction in forecast error and a 30 percent reduction in lost sales.

Those improvements are the types sought by consumer goods giant Procter & Gamble, whose CEO recently stated his goal of cutting supply-chain costs by a whopping $1 billion a year. Part of those savings will come from near-term efforts like the use of AI and the internet of things (IoT) technologies to automate warehouses and distribution centers. And other savings will come from longer-term projects, including the customized automation of product deliveries of up to seven thousand different stock-keeping units. Whether these and other initiatives will enable P&G to save the company $1 billion annually in supply-chain costs remains to be seen, but it's safe to say that AI will be playing a significant role in those efforts.

The Farms That Feed

AI technology is not only having a large impact on supply chains and the manufacturing of consumer goods and industrial machinery, but is also playing a big role in the production of food. The need for improved efficiency in the agricultural industry is huge. According to various statistics, 795 million people don't have enough food and, to keep pace with population growth, more food will be needed in the next fifty years than has been produced in the past ten thousand years combined. Both fresh water and arable soil are resources that have historically been difficult to acquire or maintain for agriculture. Precision agriculture—which leverages AI and fine-grain data about the state of crops—promises to significantly improve yield, reduce the waste of resources like water and fertilizer, and increase overall efficiency.

To be effective, precision agriculture requires a vast network of diverse IoT sensors to collect granular data. This information might include aerial images captured by satellites or drones (to detect crop distress before it's visible at ground level), environmental sensors in the field (to monitor the chemical composition of the soil, for instance), sensors mounted on farm equipment, weather forecast data, and soil databases.

To help make sense of these various data streams, Accenture has developed a new service—the Precision Agriculture Service—that deploys AI to enable better decision making with respect to pest control, fertilizer usage, and so on. The idea is to process IoT-sensor data with a machine-learning engine to provide feedback that can then be used in one of two ways. It can either go directly to a farmer, who can then implement a solution. Or it can be routed directly to a farm's digital work-management system that will then deploy the recommendations automatically. In the system, a feedback loop that incorporates up-to-date sensor data and real-time analytics can help establish a kind of self-healing farm. Farmers can be part of the loop when they approve the system's recommendations, but over time, as the system becomes more reliable, they can spend their time managing other tasks that aren't so easily automated.

AI is also enabling entirely new agricultural models, such as the "vertical farm," in which plants can be grown in thirty-foot-high stacks of trays in urban settings such as city warehouses. At one such facility in Newark, New Jersey, run by AeroFarms, data is continuously collected on temperature, humidity, carbon-dioxide levels, and other variables, and machine-learning software analyzes that information in real time to grow the crops (including kale, arugula, and mizuna plants) as efficiently as possible. According to the company, the Newark facility is expected to use 95 percent less water and 50 percent less fertilizer than traditional farms and, because the crops are grown indoors, pesticides aren't needed. AeroFarms is predicting that 2 million pounds of produce can be grown annually at the Newark vertical farm, only about fifteen miles from Manhattan.[11]

Precision agriculture is not yet widespread, but some of its technologies—the analysis of satellite data, for instance—have been used for years. The difference now is the pervasiveness of the IoT, which allows sensor data to talk to apps, and apps to talk to machine-learning-enabled systems. The ultimate goal with precision agriculture is that disparate systems can come together to produce recommendations that farmers can then act on in real time. The result is agricultural processes that produce less waste and higher yields. It's no wonder that precision-agriculture services are expected to grow to $4.55 billion by 2020.[12] As the technology becomes more widely used, the land will benefit, the farmer will benefit, and the hundreds of millions of people who need access to healthy affordable food will benefit. (See the sidebar "AI for Good: Akshaya Patra.")

AI for Good: Akshaya Patra

Akshaya Patra, an India nonprofit with the vision that "no child in India shall be deprived of education because of hunger," combines the power of AI with blockchain (a digital, decentralized, public ledger) and IoT technologies. To achieve its vision, the company's midday meal program provides one wholesome lunchtime meal to keep children sufficiently motivated and nourished to pursue their education. Since 2000, when it began by feeding 1,500 children, its operations have expanded to 1.6 million children per year in 2017; it commemorated its two-billionth meal served in 2016. Thus far, the nonprofit has demonstrated a 20 percent efficiency improvement in selected kitchens. Now feedback is digitized where once it was manually input, and blockchain is driving efficiencies in audit, attendance recording, and invoice processing. AI is used to accurately forecast demand, and IoT sensors monitor and sequence cooking processes to minimize waste and ensure consistent food quality. AI in combination with these other technologies will help Akshaya Patra expand its operations efficiently, meaning more children fed and kept in school.[a]

a. "About Us," Akshaya Patra, https://www.akshayapatra.org/about-us, accessed October 23, 2017.

The Third Wave in Manufacturing

In this chapter, we're beginning to see how artificial intelligence can change the nature of business processes. Factories and industrial settings will continue to be highly automated environments for a variety of reasons; safety and efficiency are two primary drivers. And while new automation technologies will replace some human workers, there's still plenty of space for people, as long as executives look beyond jobs displacement and begin to think differently about work. This is the *leadership* part of our MELDS framework, which we detailed in the introduction, and it calls for executives to focus on reimagining processes and new roles for employees working in the missing middle (as we'll discuss in detail in part two). And, as we've seen in this chapter, some skills are becoming more in demand, and entirely new categories of skills will be required. For example, as we will see in chapter 8, GE and the buyers of its equipment will always need maintenance workers, and they'll need those workers to be able to work well with new systems that can fuse their skills with advanced technologies in novel ways. This is the *skills* part of MELDS. Workers in these jobs will need to do what people do well: adapt to new situations and find novel, creative solutions to challenges that arise. Let the machines do the heavy lifting, the monitoring, and the monotonous tasks.

In the case of the researchers, engineers, farmers, and others, the data and analysis that AI systems provide can act as a third eye. And this is why the *data* part of MELDS is so important. Suddenly, very complex industrial or ecological systems become knowable. Engineers and managers can eliminate previously invisible inefficiencies, and they can make changes to certain aspects of a process with confidence. When you honestly assess the strengths of human and machine workers, and what they do well when they collaborate, a whole new world of possibilities emerges for running a business and designing your processes—that is, the important *mindset* part of MELDS. And by exploring those possibilities, companies can often develop novel businesses, like vertical farms. Indeed, it's through the *experimentation* part of MELDS that executives will be able to discover game-changing innovations that could potentially transform their company, if not their entire industry.

In the next chapter, we take artificial intelligence into the back office. It's where "second wave" automation is entrenched, and "third wave" AI has come as a welcome relief to many who have been working with awkward IT tools or inefficient processes. Here, too, we will see how AI and people's imaginations have been transforming seemingly mundane processes, opening up new possibilities for both efficiency and growth through human-machine collaborations.

A Brief History of AI

The driving technology behind the current era of adaptive processes is AI, which has been evolving over decades. A brief history of the technology gives some context to its current state of advanced capabilities.

The field of artificial intelligence was officially born in 1956, when a small group of computer and research scientists, organized by John McCarthy, including Claude Shannon, Marvin Minsky, and others, gathered at Dartmouth College for the first-ever conference to debate the possibility that machine intelligence could imitate human smarts.[a]

The conference, essentially an extended brainstorming session, was based on the assumption that every aspect of learning and creativity could be described so precisely that it could be mathematically modeled and therefore replicated by machines. The goals were lofty; from the event proposal: "An attempt will be made to find how to make machines use language, form, abstractions and concepts, solve kinds of problems now reserved for humans, and improve themselves." Of course, this was just the beginning.

The conference succeeded almost immediately in defining the field and unifying many of the mathematical ideas swirling around the concept of artificial intelligence. It also inspired entirely new areas of research in the decades that followed. For instance, Minsky, with Seymour Papert, wrote what was considered the foundational book on scope and limitations of neural networks,

a. "Artificial Intelligence and Life in 2030," Stanford One Hundred Year Study on Artificial Intelligence (AI100), September 2016, https://ai100.stanford.edu/sites/default/files/ai_100_report_0831fnl.pdf.

a kind of AI that uses biological neurons as its model. Other ideas like expert systems—wherein a computer contained deep stores of "knowledge" for specific domains like architecture or medical diagnosis—and natural language processing, computer vision, and mobile robotics can also be traced back to the event.

One conference participant was Arthur Samuel, an engineer at IBM who was building a computer program to play checkers. His program would assess the current state of a checkers board and calculate the probability that a given position could lead to a win. In 1959, Samuel coined the term "machine learning": the field of study that gives computers the ability to learn without being explicitly programmed. In 1961, his learning program was used to defeat the fourth-ranked checkers player in the United States. But because Samuel was modest and didn't enjoy the politics of self-promotion, it was not until after his retirement from IBM in 1966 that the significance of his machine-learning work became more widely known.[b]

In the decades after the conference, machine learning remained obscure, as other kinds of AI took center stage. In particular, researchers in the 1970s and 1980s focused on a concept of intelligence that was based on physical symbols and manipulated by logical rules. These symbolic systems, however, found no practical success at the time, and their failures led to a period known as an "AI winter."

b. John McCarthy and Ed Feigenbaum, "Arthur Samuel: Pioneer in Machine Learning," Stanford Infolab, http://infolab.stanford.edu/pub/voy/museum/samuel.html, accessed October 23, 2017.

In the 1990s, however, machine learning began to flourish as its practitioners integrated statistics and probability theory into their approaches. At the same time, the personal computing revolution began. Over the next decade, digital systems, sensors, the internet, and mobile phones would become common, providing all kinds of data for machine-learning experts to use when training these adaptive systems.

Today we think of a machine-learning application as one that builds models based on data sets that engineers or specialists use to train the system. It's a sharp contrast with traditional computer programming. Standard algorithms would follow a predetermined path set into motion by programmers' static instructions or code. A machine-learning system, conversely, can learn as it goes. With each new data set, it updates its models and the way it "sees" the world. In an era in which machines can learn and change based on their experiences and data, programmers have become less like rule makers and dictators, and more like teachers and trainers.

Now AI systems that deploy machine learning are everywhere. Banks use them for fraud detection; dating websites use them to suggest potential matches; marketers use them to try to predict who will respond favorably to an ad; and photo-sharing sites use them for automatic face recognition. We've come a long way since checkers. In 2016, Google's AlphaGo demonstrated a significant machine-learning advance. For the first time, a computer beat a human champion of Go, a game far more complex than checkers or chess. In a sign of the times, AlphaGo exhibited moves that were so unexpected that some observers deemed them to actually be creative and even "beautiful."[c]

The growth of AI and machine learning has been intermittent over the decades, but the way that they've crept into products and business operations in recent years shows that they're more than ready for prime time. According to Danny Lange, former head of machine learning at Uber, the technology has finally broken out of the research lab and is fast becoming "the cornerstone of business disruption."[d]

c. Cade Metz, "How Google's AI Viewed the Move No Human Could Understand," *Wired*, March 14, 2016, https://www.wired.com/2016/03/googles-ai -viewed-move-no-human-understand/.

d. Daniel Lange, "Making Uber Smarter with Machine Learning," presentation at Machine Learning Innovation Summit, San Francisco, June 8–9, 2016.

2

Accounting for Robots
AI in Corporate Functions

M oney laundering is a major concern for financial institutions, which can face heavy fines and stiff regulatory
restrictions for any infractions. At one large global
bank, up to ten thousand staffers were engaged in identifying
suspicious transactions and accounts that might indicate money
laundering, terrorist financing, and other illegal activities.
Aggressive monitoring was required to meet the rigid expectations of the US Department of Justice, and the incurred costs
were high, with an excessive number of false positives that the
bank had to investigate.

In response, the bank implemented a full suite of advanced
analytics tools for anti-money-laundering (AML) detection,
including machine-learning algorithms to better segment
transactions and accounts, and to set the optimal thresholds
for alerting investigators to any suspicious activity. All this is
done dynamically to incorporate the most recent data and
latest results. Moreover, the use of network analysis is helping to

uncover valuable new patterns—for example, the closeness of a business relationship between two of the bank's customers can help determine the likelihood that, if one of them is involved in illicit activity, then the other might also be involved.

Thus far, the results have been impressive. The AML system has reduced false positive alerts by as much as 30 percent, allowing staffers more time to investigate those cases requiring human judgment and compliance expertise. The system has also helped reduce the time required to investigate each alert, resulting in a dramatic 40 percent decrease in costs.

Allowing Humans to Be More Human

People rarely revel in performing repetitive or robotic tasks day in and day out. Talk to someone who's worked in a process with a lot of routine steps, and you'll learn how they relish an unusual situation that breaks up a workday or workweek. And if it gives them a chance to solve a hard problem, they feel as if they've made a difference to the organization or maybe even in someone's life. Research by Jordan Etkin of Duke University and Cassie Mogilner of the Wharton School suggests that some variety throughout a workday leads to increased happiness, likely tied to a greater sense of stimulation and productivity.[1] So, the question becomes, why continue to train people to work like robots? Why not let workers be more human? Or, as that global bank we discussed discovered, why not let staffers focus on higher-value tasks, requiring their judgment, experience, and expertise?

Our research has confirmed that in many cases, AI allows human workers to be more human. The rote nature of some administrative jobs like invoicing, bookkeeping, accounting, complaints, forms processing, and scheduling arose initially from the use of standard IT technologies that required humans to adjust to the machine limitations of the 1990s and 2000s. Human resources, IT security, and banking compliance departments all use processes that are often made up of well-defined, repetitive tasks. This was the "second wave" of business process improvement.

This chapter examines innovative improvements in enterprise processes—a trend that's been building for years but, thanks to technological advances, has only recently become viable for most organizations. We give examples that address basic questions that anyone interested in deploying AI for enterprise-wide processes should be asking. What will such work look like in this new era of business process transformation? Which tasks are best suited for humans and which are best for machines? While it's true that many organizations can immediately see significant gains when they use AI in conjunction with their existing workforce, what happens if you completely rethink your processes around ultra-smart systems? What kind of growth, services, and products become possible?

Your Office Robot

To answer those questions, let's start with a familiar process: categorizing and resolving complaints. In the past, much of the process work around sorting through customer complaints was done manually, and the tedium of many of those tasks detracted from people's job satisfaction. At Virgin Trains, a train-operating company in the UK, for example, a team of customer service reps would manually read, sort, and route complaints. These repetitive activities diverted employees' time and attention, and it fatigued them more than other work they did, like directly talking to customers.

Because the read-sort-route process is clearly defined, it is in some ways an excellent example of a process ripe for automation. But because the incoming information is text-based and is considered "unstructured" in the eyes of software systems, parsing could have been difficult for a less advanced system. Enter AI. Virgin Trains has now installed a machine-learning platform, inSTREAM, with natural-language processing capabilities that can recognize patterns in unstructured data by analyzing a corpus of similar examples—in this case, complaints—and by tracking how customer service representatives interact with incoming text.

Now when a complaint arrives at Virgin Trains, it's automatically read, sorted, and packaged into a case ready file that an employee can quickly review and process. The most common complaints get appropriate, automated responses. If the software isn't fully confident in its assessment of a complaint, it flags it as an exception for a human worker to review; the worker's response effectively updates the software's model. Over time, this kind of feedback improves the algorithm's confidence for an increasing array of scenarios. The system can handle complaints that are terse or long-winded, generic or specific, or in English or other languages.

Thanks to this new technology, Virgin Train's complaints department has decreased its manual work by 85 percent. It also increased correspondence by 20 percent because the new capabilities prompted the company to further open itself to customer interactions. Previously, the company only accepted complaints through its website. Now, it can process inquiries of any type, including email, fax, snail mail, and social media.[2] (Virgin Trains is one of many companies adding some automated intelligence to the back office; see the sidebar "AI in Business Processes" for more examples.)

AI in Business Processes

For every company and business unit and division, there are a mass of behind-the-scenes activities. The introduction of AI can help to offset the burden of repetitive, low-visibility tasks so that employees can focus on higher-value tasks.

- At Goldman Sachs, AI studies up to a million different analyst reports to identify the top factors affecting share prices.[a]

- Woodside Petroleum uses IBM's Watson to extend the sharing of lessons learned through HR, legal, and exploration.[b]

- Along with human moderators, the *Huffington Post* uses AI to flag inappropriate comments, spam, and abusive language.[c]

- Arizona State University is now using an adaptive learning tool that deploys machine learning to provide a personalized tutor for students in introductory classes.[d]

a. Nathaniel Popper, "The Robots Are Coming for Wall Street," *New York Times*, February 25, 2016, https://www.nytimes.com/2016/02/28/magazine/the -robots-are-coming-for-wall-street.html.

b. Daniel Russo, "Hiring Heroes: How Woodside Energy Works with IBM Watson," IBM Watson blog, September 11, 2017, https://www.ibm.com/blogs /watson/2017/09/hiring-heroes-woodside-energy-works-ibm-watson/.

c. Mike Masnick, "HuffPost Moderates Comments to Please Advertisers [Updated: Or Not]," *Tech Dirt*, October 30, 2012, https://www.techdirt.com /articles/20121022/12562620788/huffpost-moderates-comments-to-please -advertisers.shtml.

d. Seth Fletcher, "How Big Data Is Taking Teachers Out of the Lecturing Business," *Scientific American*, August 1, 2013, https://www.scientificamerican.com /article/how-big-data-taking-teachers-out-lecturing-business.

Moving Well Beyond RPA

The Virgin Trains system is a relatively advanced form of back-office automation because it can analyze and adapt to unstructured data as well as the sudden influx of data. Such applications are called "robotic process automation" (RPA). Simply put, RPA is software that performs digital office tasks that are administrative, repetitive, and mostly transactional within a workflow. In other words, it *automates* existing processes. But in order to *reimagine* processes, firms must utilize more advanced technologies—namely, AI. (See the sidebar "AI Technologies and Applications: How Does This All Fit Together?" at the end of this chapter.)

Now we're talking about systems that deploy AI techniques such as computer vision, or machine-learning tools to analyze unstructured or complex information. It might be able to read various styles of invoices, contracts, or purchase orders, for instance. It can process these documents—no matter the format—and put the correct values into forms and databases for further action. And then there are even more advanced systems that deploy sophisticated machine-learning algorithms not just to perform the tasks they've been programmed to do, but also to assess tasks and processes and adjust as needed. They can learn from observation by "watching over the shoulders" of human employees in order to improve their performance over time. In other words, they are exactly the kind of technology that is enabling the third wave of business process improvement—adaptable processes—that we discussed in the introduction chapter. These applications are more transformational and typically require human employees to actively participate, applying a kind of tacit knowledge or expertise that is difficult to explain or model. Think of the global bank's anti-money-laundering system that we discussed earlier. A complicated financial transaction is processed; an automated system flags it as being suspicious; and a human expert exercises the judgment to decide whether it warrants further investigation. This type of human-machine collaboration is also typical of the third wave of business process transformation.

Companies can deploy a range of these technologies, sometimes even for the same application. Case in point: Unilever's process for hiring employees. Say you're looking for a job and through LinkedIn you find a position at Unilever that might be suitable. For the first round of the application process, you'd be asked to play twelve online games based on tests from the field of cognitive neuroscience. The games help assess certain traits, like your risk aversion and ability to read emotional versus contextual cues. According to Unilever, there are no right or wrong answers to the games because, for example, an appetite for risk might be suitable for one type of job while an aversion to risk might be better for another type of position. For this round of the application process, advanced AI isn't required and a relatively basic technology like RPA would suffice.

But if you, as an applicant, made it to the next round, you'd then be asked to submit a video-recorded interview through your computer or smartphone in which you'd answer a set of questions designed for the specific position you were interested in. And here's where sophisticated AI technologies come into play: Your answers would then by analyzed by HireVue, an AI application that not only notes the words you use but also your body language and tone. The best candidates for the position are then invited to the company offices, where they can then be assessed by humans who would make the final hiring decision.

Not only does this Unilever example show how different technologies can be used for different parts of the same application; it also demonstrates the power of human-machine collaboration. Within 90 days of the new system going live, job applications had doubled to 30,000 from the same time period a year ago. In addition, the average time for someone to be hired plunged from four months to just four weeks, and the time that recruiters spent reviewing applications plummeted by 75 percent. Moreover, the company reports that, since installing the system, it has hired its most diverse class to date. For one thing, there was a dramatic increase in the universities represented, from 840 to 2,600.[3]

How Do You Know Which Processes to Change?

Repetition. Replication. Redundancy. A well-outlined process. If these elements show up in your business operations, it's a clue that tasks or processes are ready to be changed.

Roger Dickey, a developer and founder of the fast-growing startup Gigster, recognized replication and redundancy in the code of most software applications. At the same time, each new software project—regardless of how similar it was to others that had come before—was incredibly complex to build, complete with bugs and pitfalls that slowed production. Could AI be used to help reimagine the business processes required to build software?

The answer, as Gigster has found, is yes. The company typically uses AI to assess the needs of any given software project and automatically assembles an ad hoc team of crack developers to build it. If you are a small firm that needs an app or some other software product but don't have the time or resources to hire a team of developers yourself, you turn to Gigster. If you are a large corporation that doesn't want to divert resources away from established projects, you turn to Gigster.

Gigster effectively takes aim at multiple areas of the enterprise: HR (developer teams are assembled using AI), procurement (quotes are generated using AI), and IT (members of development work and are managed with AI-enabled assistance).

How does Gigster upend procurement and HR? Suppose you'd like to build an app that can help patients consolidate their medical records to share with their doctors. Where do you begin? First, you give Gigster a short document that explains the app's core function and how you envision a person will use it. On Gigster's end, the project description is cross-referenced with others in Gigster's portfolio of "data structures," which is essentially a catalog of software features. Dickey says his company has mapped the "software genome" and understands five hundred different features a product might have. Next, Gigster takes into account about twenty other customer requirements for how the user interface should look or how quickly the job needs to be completed, and so on. From the customer's mockup, description, and requirements, Gigster's AI quote generator leverages previous projects with similar constraints to estimate a price and a timeline.

If you agree to the price and timeline, the next set of Gigster's AI features goes to work. The company deploys its "team builder" in which it matches the demands of your app to members of software development teams who can meet your needs. A typical team will consist of three to five people: a project manager, a designer or two, and a developer or two, all high-performing recruits who are monitored closely by Gigster's online system, which allows the company to guarantee quality and on-time products. This initial setup takes one to three days.

Because software developers work in a digital realm, everything they do can be recorded relatively easily and analyzed. "We believe work is measurable and that data has patterns and those patterns can be exploited to find new efficiencies in work," says Dickey. This means that Gigster knows what processes go into making a software project a success—based on hundreds of other projects just like it—and an AI tool can use that information to spot potential production hiccups before they spiral out of control. Moreover, whenever developers are having trouble with any particular pieces of code, an AI assistant can automatically put them in touch with someone who's recently solved or is grappling with a similar problem. It's "an AI assistant who knows where you are in the project," says Dickey, "and can match you with other people in the world doing the same thing."[4] That type of employee augmentation is one of the keys of the third wave of human-machine collaboration.

How Do You Know How Much to Change?

By the very nature of its business—software—Gigster has been able to deploy AI to a range of IT and business processes. Other firms, however, might be better off applying AI to just a few processes. For those organizations, executives need to make judicious decisions about how best to augment their existing employees. And they also must have a plan for scaling up their use of AI in processes.

Those issues were key concerns for SEB, a major Swedish bank, which has been busy installing a virtual assistant called Amelia. Built by IPsoft, Amelia (later renamed Aida in SEB's application) now interacts directly with SEB's 1 million customers. Within the first three weeks in this role, the software held more than four thousand conversations with seven hundred people and was able to resolve the majority of the issues, says Rasmus Järborg, SEB's chief strategy officer. The decision to move Aida to a customer-facing role came only after the bank had tested the software internally as a virtual IT help-desk agent, assisting its fifteen thousand employees.[5]

Aida is adept at handling natural-language conversations, and the technology is even able to monitor a caller's tone of voice as a way to offer better service in the future. The software adapts, learning new skills by monitoring human customer-service agents. This means its capabilities improve and increase over time; new tasks and processes within the customer service department can become automated with little direct effort by the people who work there.

SEB is the first bank to use Amelia for interactions with customers, and IPsoft has helped to set up an in-house talent pool of individuals who can mentor the software. These human mentors supervise learning and performance and identify new ways to apply the technology for customer service.[6] We discuss this type of human-machine collaboration in greater detail in chapter 5.

Aida is showing that automated natural-language customer communications are possible in large and complex business environments. As natural-language techniques improve and interfaces advance, they will continue spreading throughout different business functions in various industries. In chapter 4 we'll discuss how various natural-language processing chatbots like Amazon's Alexa are becoming the new front-office faces of companies.

Redefining an Entire Industry

As AI becomes increasingly capable of adding intelligence to middle- and back-office processes, the technology could potentially redefine entire industries. In IT security, for instance, a growing number of security firms are combining machine-learning approaches to build ultra-smart, continually evolving defenses against malicious software. These systems can unearth harmful viruses and malware before they cause damage, and they can predict vulnerabilities before they become liabilities that let hackers take over entire systems. In some cases, the IT security process is a closed, automated loop; humans can step away from the day-to-day controls and spend time researching threats or creating new simulations to further test and train bots. (See the sidebar "When Bots Collide.")

In traditional cybersecurity, a company might perform analytics on existing data, gathering signatures of threats and using them to protect against future threats. It's a static operation, and not able to adapt in real time. In contrast, AI-based approaches are able to recognize anomalous patterns as they arise. They do so by calibrating models based on network traffic behavior and scoring anomalies according to the extent to which they deviate from the norm. What's more, AI-based analytics improve as each alert is eventually resolved—either by machine or human—effectively incorporating each new insight into the system as it runs.

When Bots Collide

At the 2016 DARPA Cyber Grand Challenge held in Las Vegas, it was bot versus bot in an intense battle for supremacy. Automated systems were instructed to find and exploit security holes in the software of competing machines while keeping their own systems protected.[a]

The winning bot, named Mayhem, from a Carnegie Mellon spinoff called ForAllSecure, won by deploying game theory–based tactics. Essentially, it would find its own security holes and then run a cost-benefit analysis on whether it should immediately patch them or not. (Deploying a patch required the system to take itself offline momentarily.) If an attack seemed unlikely, it was able to spend more time online, exploiting the weaknesses in other systems.

Although the bots in the competition had some quirks that indicated they were not quite ready for prime time, the experts' consensus was that the systems performed impressively, in some cases finding and fixing preplanted bugs faster than a human could. All this points to a world of automated hacking, in which humans play a decidedly different role, for example, by training bots or by ensuring their behavior doesn't cross legal or ethical bounds.

a. Cade Metz, "DARPA Goes Full *Tron* with Its Brand Battle of the Hack Bots," *Wired*, July 5, 2016, https://www.wired.com/2016/07/_trashed-19/.

Various security companies have their own approaches to the problem. SparkCognition, for instance, offers a product called Deep Armor, which uses a combination of AI techniques including neural networks, heuristics, data science, and natural-language processing to detect threats never seen before and remove malicious files. Another company called Darktrace offers a product called Antigena, which is modeled on the human immune system, identifying and neutralizing bugs as they're encountered.[7] Behavioral analysis of network traffic is key to another company called Vectra. Its AI-enabled software learns the signatures of malicious network behavior and can deploy automated actions to squelch the attack, or pass it off to a team of security experts, who can also decide how to handle attacks.[8]

Reimagining Processes Around People

AI technology promises to offload dull and tedious office tasks to software robots, resulting in a work environment that can offer greater satisfaction to human workers. This is the "missing middle" of human-machine symbiotic collaboration that we described in our introductory chapter. It's where companies can generate the most value—more so than with automation—from investments in advanced digital technologies.

In this chapter, we saw the *leadership* part of MELDS in action as one global bank was able to reimagine its process for detecting money laundering by using machine-learning algorithms to reduce the number of false positives so that human experts could focus on the more complex, suspicious cases. That type of business process relies heavily on good data, and many companies have been discovering the power of tapping into multiple sources. In the past, Virgin Trains could handle complaints only through its website, but now the company has invested in the *data* part of MELDS, enabling it to deploy a natural-language processing application that can accept customer inquiries from a variety of channels, including social media. As such systems are deployed, though, employees will need to adjust how they work, and companies must devote resources to the *skills* part of MELDS. At Gigster, for instance, we saw how AI assistants can automatically put a program developer in touch with others who are grappling with a similar problem, which thus places a premium on the collaborative capabilities of employees. Another lesson from this chapter was that the path toward filling the missing middle takes time as, for example, companies move from RPA to advanced AI, and that transition requires experimentation. The Swedish bank SEB paid proper attention to the *experimentation* part of MELDS by conducting extensive tests of its virtual assistant Aida on its fifteen thousand employees before launching the system to its one million customers. And lastly, we learned about the importance of the *mindset* part of MELDS as we saw the potential power of AI to transform an entire industry like IT security, with automated systems helping to uncover malware and identify vulnerabilities so that they can be addressed before a system is breached.

In chapter 3, we'll see how that middle zone can also be extended to the R&D process itself. There, as with the factory floor and office, savvy companies have been reaping the rewards of smart, complementary collaborations between man and machine.

AI Technologies and Applications: How Does This All Fit Together?

Here is a glossary of the constellation of AI technologies you need to know about today. These technologies correspond to the machine learning, AI capabilities, and AI applications layers of figure 2-1.[a]

Machine Learning Component

Machine learning (or ML). The field of computer science that deals with algorithms that learn from and make predictions on data without needing to be explicitly programmed. The field has its roots in the research of Arthur Samuel of IBM, who in 1959 coined the term and used ML principles in his work on computer games. Thanks to the explosion of available data for training these algorithms, ML is now used in fields as diverse and sprawling as vision-based research, fraud detection, price prediction, natural language processing, and more.

Supervised learning. A type of ML in which an algorithm is presented with preclassified and sorted data (known in the field as "labeled data") consisting of example inputs and desired outputs. The goal for the algorithm is to learn the general rules that connect the inputs to the outputs and use those rules to predict future events with input data alone.

a. Accenture Research; Jerry Kaplan, *Artificial Intelligence: What Everyone Needs to Know* (New York, Oxford University Press: 2016); and Wikipedia, s.v. "Artificial intelligence," https://en.wikipedia.org/wiki/Artificial_intelligence.

FIGURE 2-1

The constellation of AI technologies and business applications

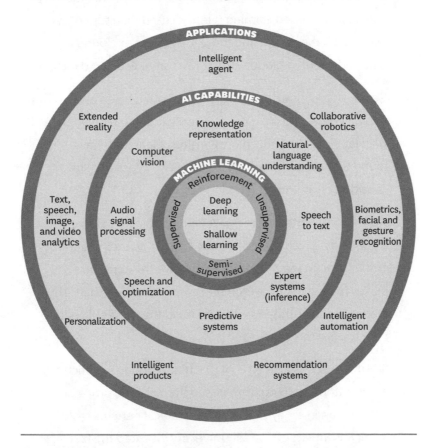

Unsupervised learning. No labels are given to the learning algorithm, leaving it to find the structures and patterns of the inputs on its own. Unsupervised learning can be a goal in itself (discovering hidden patterns in data), or a means toward an end (extracting features within the data). Unsupervised learning is less focused than supervised learning on the output and more focused on exploring input data and inferring hidden structures from unlabeled data.

Semi-supervised learning. Uses both labeled and unlabeled data for training—typically more unlabeled data than labeled. Many machine learning researchers have found that the combination of these two types of data considerably improves learning accuracy.

Reinforcement learning. A kind of training in which an algorithm is given a specific goal, such as operating a robot arm or playing the game Go. Each move the algorithm makes toward the goal is either rewarded or punished. The feedback allows the algorithm to build the most efficient path toward the goal.

Neural network. A type of machine learning in which an algorithm, learning from observational data, processes information in a way similar to a biological nervous system. Frank Rosenblatt of Cornell University invented the first neural network, a simple, single-layer architecture (also known as a shallow network) in 1957.

Deep learning and subsets: deep neural networks (DNN), recurrent neural networks (RNN), and feedforward neural networks (FNN). A set of techniques to train a multilayered neural network. In a DNN, "sensed" data is processed through multiple layers; each layer uses the output of the previous layer as its input. RNNs allow the data to flow back and forth through the layers, in contrast to FNNs, in which data may only flow one way.

AI Capabilities Component

Predictive systems. A system that finds relationships between variables in historical data sets and their outcomes. The relationships are used to develop models, which in turn are used to predict future outcomes.

Local search (optimization). A mathematical approach to problem solving that uses an array of possible solutions. The algorithm searches for an optimal solution by starting at one point in the array and iteratively and systematically moving to neighboring solutions until it finds the optimal solution.

Knowledge representation. A field of artificial intelligence dedicated to representing information about the world in a form that a computer system can use to perform complex tasks such as diagnosing disease or conducting a conversation with a person.

Expert systems (inference). A system that uses field-specific knowledge (medicine, chemistry, legal) combined with a rules engine that dictates how that knowledge is applied. The system improves as more knowledge is added or when the rules are updated and improved.

Computer vision. A field that focuses on teaching computers to identify, categorize, and understand the content within images and video, mimicking and extending what the human visual system does.

Audio and signal processing. Machine learning that can be used to analyze audio and other digital signals, especially in high-noise environments. Applications include computational speech, and audio and audiovisual processing.

Speech to text. Neural networks that convert audio signals to text signals in a variety of languages. Applications include translation, voice command and control, audio transcription, and more.

Natural language processing (NLP). A field in which computers process human (natural) languages. Applications include speech recognition, machine translation, and sentiment analysis.

AI Applications Component

Intelligent agents. Agents that interact with humans via natural language. They can be used to augment human workers working in customer service, human resources, training, and other areas of business to handle FAQ-type inquiries.

Collaborative robotics (cobots). Robots that operate at slower speeds and are fitted with sensors to enable safe collaboration with human workers.

Biometrics, facial, and gesture recognition. Identifies people, gestures, or trends in biometric measures (stress, activity, etc.) for purposes of natural human-machine interaction, or identification and verification.

Intelligent automation. Transfers some tasks from man to machine to fundamentally change the traditional ways of operating. Through machine-specific strengths and capabilities (speed, scale, and the ability to cut through complexity), these tools complement human work to expand what is possible.

Recommendation systems. Make suggestions based on subtle patterns detected by AI algorithms over time. These can be targeted toward consumers to suggest new products or used internally to make strategic suggestions.

Intelligent products. Have intelligence baked into their design so that they can evolve to continuously meet and anticipate customers' needs and preferences.

Personalization. Analyzes trends and patterns for customers and employees to optimize tools and products for individual users or customers.

Text, speech, image, and video recognition. Parses text, speech, image, and video data and creates associations that can be used to scale analytical activities and enable higher-level applications related to interaction and vision.

Extended reality. Combines the power of AI with virtual, augmented, and mixed-reality technology to add intelligence to training, maintenance, and other activities.

3

The Ultimate
Innovation Machine

AI in R&D and Business Innovation

Automaker Tesla has been breaking ground in many ways. Obviously, the company is well known for its snazzy (and pricey) automobiles—including the Tesla Roadster, the first electric sports car—which have attracted not only customers but investors as well. In spring 2017, Tesla's market capitalization topped $50 billion, slightly edging the value of General Motors.[1] But it's not just the company's stylish, electric vehicles and soaring stock price that are noteworthy; it's also the clever ways in which the firm conducts its research and development.

In 2016, Tesla announced that every new vehicle would be equipped with all the hardware it needs to drive autonomously, including a bevy of sensors and an onboard computer running a neural network.[2] The kicker: the autonomous AI software won't be fully deployed. As it turns out, Tesla will test drivers against software simulations running in the background on the car's computer. Only when the background program consistently simulates moves more safely than the driver does will the autonomous software be ready for prime time. At that point, Tesla will release the program through remote software updates. What this all means is that Tesla drivers will, in aggregate, be teaching the fleet of cars how to drive.

Tesla is training its AI platform in a distributed test bed with the best data around—its own drivers in real-life conditions. In this case, people's driving skills—at scale—are crucial in the training of the system. AI has allowed Tesla to rethink its fundamental R&D processes and, along the way, speed up the development of its system. This reconsideration of how it conducts R&D is positioning Tesla to be a leader in autonomous cars.

Tesla isn't the only one using AI to rethink its R&D processes, using both machines and people in new, innovative ways. This chapter explores the way that AI enables experimentation within companies and how it's shaking up business processes, especially those that involve customers, medical patients, and others who provide useful data.

You'll see how AI is boosting R&D in the pharmaceutical and life sciences industries, augmenting researchers' intuition and ability to test theories, and speeding up the product-design cycle by orders of magnitude. Thanks to the glut of customer and patient data, traditional processes for researching and developing products and services are changing. Where finding a mass-market hit was once a company's primary driver, ultra-customization is becoming an increasingly critical—and economically feasible—approach.

The Augmented Researcher: How Science Works in the Age of AI

First, we need to step back to understand some basic principles. The scientific method is perhaps the most well-understood, widely deployed process in the world. Over centuries, it has come to be defined as a series of discrete, reproducible steps. First, ask questions and make observations. Next, devise hypotheses. After that, design an experiment to test predictions based on the hypotheses. Then, of course, run tests and collect data. Finally, develop generalized theories. As a process, the scientific method can be visualized cyclically. All that data and those general theories lead to more observation and further research, getting the ball rolling all over again.

Because the scientific method's steps are so clear-cut, it's no surprise that there are opportunities for artificial intelligence to change the shape of the process itself. While, so far, research institutions and companies involved in science have not fully overhauled the way science is done, some have successfully compressed or exploded particular scientific steps. The following sections look at AI disruptions at each stage of the scientific process—considering which tasks are best for people, which are best for machines, and how both work together.

Opportunities in Observation

Isaac Asimov contended that "the most exciting phrase to hear in science, the one that heralds new discoveries, is not 'Eureka!,' but 'that's funny . . .'"[3] The observation phase of the scientific process is full of twists and turns and unexpected paths as scientists pore over the latest research, stumble upon a surprise chemical reaction, or through a serendipitous conversation with a colleague, arrive at a new research question.

But now think about how challenging scientific observation is in the modern era; there are already so many studies to consider and so much data to sort. Research from the University of Ottawa in 2009 noted that the total number of science papers published since 1665 exceeds 50 million, and more than 2.5 million new scientific papers are published annually.[4] And that's just the papers. What about all the raw data—structured, unstructured, cataloged, cleaned, sifted, and analyzed? Our digital lives produce staggering amounts of data each day. What kind of observations could be done with that? How might we even arrive at the point where something seems "funny" or worth exploring further? (See the sidebar "Learning from Failure.")

While human researchers are very good at creative insights, machines are unequivocally better at data organization and presentation, especially when data volume becomes unwieldy. One company, called Quid, is using AI to reimagine the search-and-find part of the researchers' process. Quid's platform uses natural-language processing to create data visualizations from large bodies of text data—from patents to news reports—and sorts the text into networks of ideas. The company's interface, best experienced on a touchscreen, reveals concepts, clusters, and clumps of similarity as well as strong and tenuous connections between ideas.

Shivon Zilis, an investor at Bloomberg Beta, uses Quid in a number of aspects of her work. Zilis might spend her day developing a thesis for the next emerging tech trend, sourcing deals, or helping guide the development of companies she invests in.

Learning from Failure

At Haverford College in Pennsylvania, chemistry researchers used machine learning to extract insight from data of both failed and successful experiments. Specifically, the researchers considered nearly four thousand crystal-producing chemical reactions logged in the lab over a decade, including "dark" reactions that had been attempted but didn't pan out. Once the data was sorted—nearly three hundred properties were attributed to each reaction—a machine-learning algorithm went to work trying to make connections between conditions that led to crystal growth.

The algorithm was able to predict crystals in 89 percent of the cases, besting the researchers (who used intuition and experience alone) who did so in 78 percent of cases. What's more, the algorithm used a decision-tree model, which produced a kind of branched flow chart of each successive move, so the researchers could inspect the logic of its decisions. Thanks to this transparency, the researchers used the experiment to formulate new hypotheses.[a]

a. Paul Raccuglia et al., "Machine-Learning-Assisted Materials Discovery Using Failed Experiments," *Nature*, May 4, 2016, 73–76.

Without a tool like Quid, Zilis would have to rely on a hodgepodge of tactics to do her research—searching Google using a variety of search terms or reading news from a necessarily limited number of sources, for instance. But with Quid, Zilis can visualize trends that emerge from analysis of a more complete set of news sources. She can notice connections between technologies that might have been obscured otherwise. Moreover, Zilis's finely tuned research intuition is amplified, which gives her more opportunities to ask additional questions and follow unusual threads as she zooms in and out of the visualized network of ideas. What Quid gives an investor, essentially, is a platform for a next-level observation—questions come quicker and they are more nuanced and incisive—and that can open the gates to unexpected avenues of inquiry, leading to a smarter hypothesis.[5]

The Smart, Automated Hypothesis

After observation, scientists form hypotheses, essentially a proposed—and testable—explanation for a phenomenon. What happens to the scientific process when hypotheses can be generated automatically? The precision medicine company GNS Healthcare is exploring that possibility. Its powerful machine learning and simulation software, Reverse Engineering and Forward Simulation (REFS), can churn out hypotheses straight from the data to find relationships in patients' medical health records. In one instance, GNS was able to recreate in three months the results of a two-year-long study on drug interactions.

The study involved finding adverse reactions between drug combinations by seniors using Medicare. Bad drug combinations are a major problem without a standard solution: drugs aren't tested in combination in US Food and Drug Administration trials, so there's no easy way to see which ones are dangerous when combined. Historically, researchers might have relied on scientific intuition to notice that drugs that operate via similar enzymatic pathways might interact adversely with other drugs in a similar way. Next, researchers might have developed the hypothesis—for example, drug A plus drug B is leading to adverse event C—and then, of course, they'd test it. Using such an approach, researchers would have discovered that two common drugs for seniors interact poorly, but the study took two years to develop and confirmed only the limited hypothesis about interaction between just those two drugs.

In a test of the REFS system, GNS assessed anonymous data from about 200,000 patients and a wide array of drugs on the market. The data itself was encrypted, says GNS's chairman, cofounder, and CEO Colin Hill. "We had no knowledge of what the drugs were. There was no way we could cheat."[6] The machine-learning platform churned through approximately 45 quadrillion hypotheses, and after only three months, the combination of drugs most likely to lead to troublesome interactions emerged as a final result.

Hill says that the people on his team didn't know if their results were right or not; they simply handed them over to researchers studying drug interactions. As it turned out, REFS did indeed uncover the drug interaction that had taken two years to confirm. But it did something else as well: it also uncovered a drug interaction that had only been discussed among patients, but wasn't formally studied. The researchers were able to examine their own observational data on those drugs from a year prior and then look at the records to see what the interactions were a year later. There, in their own records, was validation of a causal connection, hidden in plain sight. "It was the first time that I know of that machines discovered new medical knowledge," says Hill. "Straight from the data. There was no human involved in this discovery."[7]

GNS Healthcare is showing that it's possible, when AI is injected into the hypothesis phase of the scientific method, to find previously hidden correlations and causations. Moreover, use of the technology can result in dramatic cost savings. In one recent success, GNS was able to reverse-engineer—without using a hypothesis or preexisting assumptions—PCSK9, a class of drug that reduces bad cholesterol in the bloodstream. It took seventy years to discover PCSK9 and tens of billions of dollars over decades. But using the same starting data only, GNS's machine-learning models were able to recreate all the known LDL biology in less than ten months for less than $1 million.

Exploding the Design Space

After the hypothesis comes tests. For many companies, this stage is intimately tied to product design. Here, firms can use AI and big data to scope out myriad alternatives and then narrow the scope of their experiment to select for the most likely candidates. It's a recurring story: AI helps organizations refocus resources—and most fundamentally, their human resources—into higher-value activities.

Consider Nike, which recently turned to AI for the specific problem of making better spikes for sprinters. The challenge: a stiff spike plate is better—giving runners something solid to push off against—but the most common way to achieve stiffness is to use heavier materials. Unfortunately, heavy materials weigh a sprinter down.

With the help of the company's algorithmic design software, Nike designers optimized for both stiffness and lightness, conceiving a shoe from scratch. Human designers alone would have likely started from existing shoes and iterated until they found something that was satisfactory, but not nearly as optimized. In the end, the company was able to 3-D print various prototypes and test them, and repeat the cycle until it found the premier design. The ultimate shoe can shave a tenth of a second off a sprinter's time, which can be the difference between first and fourth place. Nike's rapid prototyping of shoe designs points to the way AI disrupts the next phase of the scientific process. Intelligent algorithms are compressing the time it takes to test.[8] (For additional examples of AI in product design, see the sidebar "AI in Product and Service Design.")

Faster Testers

Many researchers find that their least favorite part of what they do is actually running an experiment and collecting the data. The other parts of the R&D process—discovery and asking questions—provide them the most satisfaction. It's a relief, then, to realize what a boon artificial intelligence is to experimental testing. Here we see another recurring story: AI can resolve the tedium and allow practitioners to bypass drudgery, to spend more time conceiving new experiments, for instance, or asking unexpected questions. The business benefit is clear: bringing more high-quality products to market faster.

While today's experimental environments look, in some fundamental ways, similar to labs from decades ago—mice in cages, petri dishes in incubators, titration systems, and so on—many areas of science are moving more fully into silicon. That is, they can simulate experiments inside computers. In chapter 1, we described GE's software Predix, which runs virtual experiments with digitized versions of factory machines. But the reality is, you don't need Predix to create a model of your processes and run tests. You just need a solid understanding of the steps in your process and clean data that you can use to develop a model.

AI in Product and Service Design

The internet, with all the customer data it gathers and communication it fosters, has been responsible for a phase shift in the way that companies improve their products and services. AI now enables even more rapid analysis of customer preferences, allowing for personalized and customizable experiences.

- IntelligentX Brewing Company bills its products as the first beer brewed by AI. It translates its customer feedback, directed through Facebook Messenger, into recipe changes, which affect the brew composition over time.[a]

- Lenovo uses text-mining tools to listen to customers voicing their problems worldwide. Insights from discussions of those problems then feed into product and service improvements.[b]

- Las Vegas Sands Corp. uses AI to model different layouts of gaming stations throughout its casino to optimize financial performance. By monitoring how different layouts affect profits, the company gains continuous insights that inform future renovations.[c]

a. Billy Steele, "AI Is Being Used to Brew Beer in the UK," *Engadget*, July 7, 2016, https://www.engadget.com/2016/07/07/intelligentx-brewing-beer-with-ai/.

b. Rebecca Merrett, "How Lenovo Uses Text Analytics for Product Quality and Design," *CIO*, September 2, 2015, https://www.cio.com.au/article/583657/how-lenovo-uses-text-analytics-product-quality-design/.

c. Ed Burns, "Analytical Technologies Are Game Changer for Casino Company," *SearchBusinessAnalytics*, October 2014, http://searchbusinessanalytics.techtarget.com/feature/Analytical-technologies-are-game-changer-for-casino-company.

Everything from financial services and insurance products to beer brewing and shaving-cream chemistry can be described digitally. Once it is, it can be optimized. Traditionally, optimization algorithms have been confined to academia or used only by experts. One startup called SigOpt, however, realized that machine learning could turn any digital model into an easily solved optimization problem, essentially democratizing this powerful computational tool for the masses.

"You don't want to have to be an expert in Bayesian optimization in order to apply these types of techniques," says Scott Clark, CEO of SigOpt. The company's goal is to free subject-matter experts from having to spend time tweaking digital systems, trying to find best-case scenarios. Instead, it wants to empower them to experiment more.

"A chemist who is actually brewing stuff up on their lab bench can just have their laptop open or have [SigOpt's interface] on their phone," explains Clark. The software would prompt the chemist: "This is the next experiment to try." Or it might note that a certain experiment did particularly well. "It's guiding them through that as easily as possible, so they don't have to have any internal knowledge of the system" says Clark. "They just get the best results out."[9] In other words, one of the scientist's main tasks—to test ideas—is augmented by SigOpt's tools.

Personalized Delivery: Theory and Practice

After testing, scientists develop their general theories and then start the process, beginning with observation, all over again. In business, after the tests and optimization come marketing and product delivery.

Responsible AI: Ethics as a Precursor to Discovery

A significant portion of research is conducted using human subjects. To protect those individuals, many organizations have established institutional review boards (IRBs): committees that approve, monitor, and review research conducted on humans. Although IRBs are required of all research affiliated with universities in the United States, they're virtually nonexistent in the commercial world. But some companies, including Facebook, have taken it upon themselves to develop their own sets of rules regarding their research ethics committees.[a] These rules borrow from common IRB protocols but can differ in terms of transparency and the affiliations of people allowed to serve on the committees.

But what makes all of this even more challenging is that, with the exception of the pharmaceutical industry, there's no standard protocol for determining which new technology product is a human research study or how exactly a company

a. Mike Orcutt, "Facebook's Rules for Experimenting on You," *MIT Technology Review*, June 15, 2016, https://www.technologyreview.com/s/601696/facebooks-rules-for-experimenting-on-you/.

Many trends—including the increasing availability of customer data—are leading to a new level of product customization and delivery. As we saw in chapter 1, AI is making it more economical to make personalized consumables like cars. From chapter 2, we saw how AI can turn routine back-office interactions into more personalized services that improve customer experience. AI is also operating in the R&D departments responsible for should proceed as it tests and develops the product. Clearly, there are a variety of ethical gray areas when it comes to technology deployment generally and AI in particular. Facebook itself raised many ethical concerns when, in one experiment, the company manipulated what people saw on their feeds—increasing the number of positive or negative posts—to see how that would affect their moods. This prompted a *Forbes* columnist to ask, "So is it okay for Facebook to play mind games with us for science?"[b]

In part two, we explore various issues relating to the ethics of using AI in R&D and other areas. We'll see in chapter 5 how some companies are adding new job functions, such as that of the *ethics compliance manager*, who will be the official corporate watchdog and ombudsman for ensuring that the organization follows generally accepted norms of human values and morals.

b. Kashmir Hill, "Facebook Manipulated 689,003 Users' Emotions for Science," *Forbes*, June 28, 2014, https://www.forbes.com/sites/kashmirhill/2014/06/28/facebook-manipulated-689003-users-emotions-for-science/.

these changes in mass customization. (For a brief discussion of the balance between personalization and privacy, see side bar "Responsible AI: Ethics as a Precursor to Discovery.")

Take, for example, the health-care industry. AI is now enabling the era of "personalized medicine" based on genetic testing. In the past, it was virtually impossible to analyze and manage all the combinations of possible treatments for each patient by hand. Today, intelligent systems are taking over that job. Decades from now (or sooner), it will seem absurd that doctors prescribed the same treatment to a wide swath of their patients. Everyone's treatments will be personalized.

Along these lines, GNS, the analytics firm, has been crunching huge amounts of data to match specific drugs and nondrug interventions to individual patients. By better matching drugs to different individuals, the company can improve outcomes, lower costs, and save hundreds of billions of dollars, according to cofounder Hill. Now that so much data about patients' individual genomes and responsiveness to various chemical compounds is available, it simply doesn't make sense to deploy one-size-fits-all treatments. Individualized treatments could solve an especially critical problem in clinical trials, of which more than 80 percent fail due to some level of mismatching between patient and drug.[10]

The R&D Risk Factor

The use of AI in the different stages of R&D—observations, hypothesis generation, experiment design, and so on—is producing remarkable gains at all levels and in a variety of fields. Discoveries made over the course of a decade are being replicated, without any guidance, within a matter of months, resulting in dramatic time and cost savings. This has led to a fundamental rethinking of how companies manage their R&D activities.

In the past, at many firms, most R&D projects didn't pan out, meaning losses of tens of millions of dollars or more every year.

The result was that companies tended to be risk averse, less likely to fund blue-sky research projects. But when you add AI into the R&D pipeline, you speed up the discovery process for some projects and improve the success rate of others. More money can then be freed up for riskier—and potentially the most lucrative or groundbreaking—research initiatives.

The pharmaceutical industry is a case in point. Traditionally, drug discovery has started with the medicinal chemist, people who are good at looking at a pharmaceutical problem and finding molecules to match. "Unfortunately, they can only ever test maybe 1 percent of those ideas," explains Brandon Allgood, chief technology officer and cofounder of Numerate. "They have to go through a triage system of winnowing down ideas they think they can try. A lot of that is subjective. A lot of that is based on rules of thumb."[11]

Numerate deploys machine learning to identify compounds with the highest probability of success against specific disease targets. Using that technology, researchers were able to develop a better HIV drug in six months, instead of the ten years and $20 million to develop the current HIV drug. "What our machine learning allows them to do is encode all of these really good ideas to help them be able to search a billion molecules and only make a hundred or two hundred," Allgood says. "It allows them to explore many ideas that they wouldn't even get to—what I would call 'kooky' ideas—and be able to test those now because they can . . . It allows them to be more creative and allows them to think more broadly and try out different ideas."[12] (For additional examples of AI used in health-care R&D, see the sidebar "AI in Health Care and Life Sciences.")

AI in Health Care and Life Sciences

In the health-care industry, AI allows scientists and doctors to focus on high-value work to improve patients' lives.

- Berg Health uses AI to analyze patient data and create a "molecular map," which determines the likelihood that pancreatic cancer patients will respond positively to Berg's phase-two treatment.[a]

- Researchers from Cincinnati Children's Hospital are using machine learning to better predict patient participation response for clinical trials. The current participation rate is about 60 percent, but they hope to use AI to boost this to 72 percent.[b]

- Johnson & Johnson is training IBM's Watson to rapidly read and analyze scientific literature to save scientists' time in the drug discovery process.[c]

a. Meghana Keshavan, "Berg: Using Artificial Intelligence for Drug Discovery," *MedCity News*, July 21, 2015, https://medcitynews.com/2015/07/berg-artificial-intelligence/.

b. "Scientists Teaching Machines to Make Clinical Trials More Successful," Cincinnati Children's press release, April 27, 2016, https://www.cincinnatichildrens.org/news/release/2016/clinical-trials-recruitment-4-27-2016.

c. "IBM Watson Ushers in a New Era of Data-Driven Discoveries," IBM press release, August 28, 2014, https://www-03.ibm.com/press/us/en/pressrelease/44697.wss.

Smarter R&D with Intelligent Systems

In every step of the R&D process, AI is giving researchers and product developers a remarkable boost. It's changing the way people think about conceiving their experiments, freeing them up to explore avenues that might previously have been off limits because they would have required too much time and money. In this chapter, we saw how a company like Tesla is using AI to reimagine the way it develops and tests a future generation of driverless vehicles—the *experimentation* part of MELDS. AI is also enabling researchers to mine the *data* from past tests to uncover new insights and to conduct virtual experiments to test any hypothesis more quickly. All this, however, requires a shift in the employee *skills* needed, the S in MELDS. For example, when product developers can run a digital simulation to test a new design, thus freeing them from the cost, time, and tedium of having to build a physical prototype, they then must become better at conceiving more innovative products. Thanks to AI, that type of fundamental change in *mindset*—pursuing ideas that might initially lack promise but could lead to a breakthrough— has already been occurring in the pharmaceutical industry. Yet, as companies increasingly deploy AI tools to reimagine their R&D processes, *leaders* (the L part of MELDS) need to always be mindful of the ethical issues involved, especially when human subjects are involved.

The next chapter moves from R&D to marketing and sales. There we'll discover that the impact of AI has been just as great—if not more so—as machine-learning technologies like Apple's Siri and Amazon's Alexa increasingly become the digital embodiment of those company's well-known brands.

4

Say Hello to Your New Front-Office Bots

AI in Customer Service, Sales, and Marketing

Coca-Cola, the consumer beverage giant, operates a vast army of 16 million cooler cabinets keeping its soft drinks refrigerated at retail outlets worldwide.[1] This army requires thousands of employees to visit those sites and manually take stock of the Coca-Cola products at those locations. Recently, the company has been piloting a proof-of-concept project using AI to manage the coolers. The project calls for the deployment of a new AI capability, called Einstein, from customer relationship management (CRM) vendor Salesforce, which uses computer vision, deep learning, and natural-language-processing technologies.

Using an Einstein-powered app, in pilot with select Coca-Cola retailers, an employee on-site could take a cellphone photo of the cooler cabinet, and Einstein's image-recognition services will analyze the photo to identify and count the different Coca-Cola bottles in it. Einstein would then predict and recommend a restocking order, using CRM data and other information, including weather forecasts, promotional offers, inventory levels, and historical data to account for seasonal fluctuations and various other factors. The automation of the count and restocking order could save employees paperwork and time, and the added intelligence of the system has the potential to improve sales and increase customer satisfaction.

In the front office, AI is poised to help companies like Coca-Cola improve the experiences and outcomes for every critical customer interaction, including interactions in three key functions: sales, marketing, and customer service. In those areas, AI has been both automating employee tasks and augmenting workers' own capabilities. We have seen, for example, how AI agents like Amazon's Alexa and other systems that automate customer interactions now allow workers to handle more complicated tasks, and let businesses shift workers to where people skills are more important.

Such shifts are also significantly affecting the customer relationship with corporations and brands. In many cases, it can save a customer time and effort and can help provide customizable experiences and products—cutting back on a lot of (wasted) advertising—an increasingly important trend in retail. In other cases, such as digital lending—which uses AI to analyze vast and varied data troves—customers who might have been overlooked with a traditional credit check could suddenly have much easier access to credit and loans.

And finally, these changes are bound to affect the relationships that customers and brands have with the products themselves.

As consumable items produce more data about their performance and send this data back to their manufacturer, companies can start to think differently about product support and the products themselves. For instance, Philips smart lighting uses AI to predict when bulbs will lose their efficiency, which ties into the company's recycling and replacement service. In short, sensor data and AI are now allowing the company to sell "light as a service" instead of just bulbs.[2]

Heady times, for sure. But as AI enters the front office, new questions about best practices arise. How do AI and new modes of human-machine interaction change the way companies deliver goods and services, and how are these interactions shaping the future of work? How do the new user interfaces like Alexa change the relationships between companies' brands and their customers? What design choices can make or break a natural-language bot? And what happens when logos and mascots—traditional brand ambassadors—gain intelligence? These questions are at the heart of this chapter.

Customer-Aware Shops

To begin answering those questions, let's return to the retail floor. While Coca-Cola has been piloting the use of AI to automate its product-ordering process, other companies are focusing more on improving the customer experience by *augmenting* the work of floor sales staff. Take, for example, the global fashion company Ralph Lauren, which has partnered with Oak Labs, a San Francisco–based startup, to develop an integrated commerce experience for shoppers.[3] A key part of the technology is the connected fitting room, equipped with a smart mirror that relies on RFID to automatically recognize the items that a shopper brings into the room.

The mirror, which can translate six languages, can then display details about an item. It can also change the lighting (bright natural light, sunset, club setting, and so on) so shoppers can see how they look in different settings. And the mirror can indicate whether items are available in additional colors or sizes, which a sales associate delivers to the dressing room. This last feature is the kind of personalized customer service that a sales associate, harried by tending to many customers at once, usually wouldn't be able to provide.

Of course, the smart mirror also collects data about the customer—the length of a fitting-room session, the conversion ratio (items bought versus those tried on), and other information—that a store can then analyze in aggregate to gain valuable insights. For example, customers might bring a certain clothing item into the fitting room frequently, but then seldom purchase it, prompting a store to revise its future buying. And further down the line, this kind of customer data and other information such as customer movement could be used to design stores in new ways. Imagine being able to run a variety of customer-data models through design software, optimizing store layout for customer satisfaction, return visits, or the purchase of particular items.

A retailer can also use AI to address operational issues like staffing. One global Japanese clothing retailer has been working to optimize its team of sales associates on the floor. In clothing or shoe stores, salespeople are key: around 70 percent of surveyed customers report wanting in-store recommendations.[4] Thus, to make better staffing decisions, this retailer decided to use a system from an AI company called Percolata.

The software developed an optimal schedule, in fifteen-minute increments, for the stores, and suggested the most effective combination of sales associates at any one time. The automation eliminated managers' sometimes inadvertent biases in scheduling "favorites" more often, even if they didn't contribute to the overall success of a sales team. In a rollout of the system in twenty US locations, the company discovered that its stores were overstaffed 53 percent of the time and understaffed 33 percent of the time, and Percolata's scheduling recommendations have boosted the Japanese retailer's sales by 10 to 30 percent.[5] In addition, Percolata's system frees managers from an estimated three hours daily that they had previously used for fiddling with schedules, and it allows sales workers more flexibility in their hours.

An innovation from Europe is pushing the retail envelope in other ways. Almax, an Italian company, has developed a mannequin with computer vision and facial-recognition technology.[6] The AI system can identify you by your gender, approximate age, and race. Boutique shops and fashion brands like Benetton have been deploying the high-tech mannequins to learn more about their customers. One retail outlet, for example, discovered that men who shopped during the first few days of a sale tended to spend more than women, prompting that business to modify its window displays accordingly. Another store reportedly learned that Chinese shoppers made up one-third of customers using a particular entrance after 4 p.m., so Chinese-speaking staffers were located there during these hours.

In the future, retailers could use AI technology to provide customer personalization—a mannequin or mirror that recognizes you can pull up your buying history and help a human salesclerk suggest articles of clothing that you might like. Such advances would typify the human-machine collaboration and augmentation described in the introductory chapter, with AI technology doing what it does best (sifting through and processing copious data to recommend certain actions) and humans doing what they do best (exercising their judgment and social skills to help customers purchase products that better fit their needs). Moreover, as AI systems become more advanced, they will be able to analyze a customer's facial expression and voice tone to determine that person's emotional state, and then respond in the appropriate way. In chapter 5, we'll see how some advanced AI applications are already being trained to be more empathetic. (For additional examples of how retailers are currently taking advantage of AI to personalize the shopping experience online and in stores, see the sidebar "AI in Retail Sales.")

However, as such technological advances continue pushing the retail envelope, they'll likely raise privacy and ethical concerns. Almax, for instance, has been working to extend its mannequins' hearing capability, raising fears they can potentially eavesdrop to capture customers' reactions to the clothing displayed. In chapter 5, we'll discuss how companies that deploy such cutting-edge technologies will need human employees to assess and address the various ethical concerns likely to arise.

AI for Super Salespeople

AI is not only helping salespeople on the retail floor; it's also empowering them wherever and whenever they're interacting with customers. From automatically sending perfectly composed emails via a digital assistant to cleverly and quickly organizing sales data, AI is offloading some of the major time sinks of sales teams. What's

AI in Retail Sales

Recent studies belie the once-feared demise of brick-and-mortar stores due to online retailers. Now with AI, both channels can better personalize the shopping experience.

- Lowe's "Lowebot" is a physical robot that maneuvers around stores in eleven retail locations in the San Francisco area, answering shoppers' questions and checking stock levels on shelves.[a]

- H&M, partnering with the popular chat platform Kik, has developed a bot plug-in that, based on a short questionnaire, suggests clothing items and learns style preferences over time.[b]

- The Kraft Phone Assistant gives "recipes of the day" and identifies ingredients and where to buy them. Over time, it learns preferences, such as favorite stores and the number of people in a household, to refine its recommendations.[c]

a. Harriet Taylor, "Lowe's Introduces LoweBot, a New Autonomous In-Store Robot," *CNBC*, August 30, 2016, https://www.cnbc.com/2016/08/30/lowes-introduces-lowebot-a-new-autonomous-in-store-robot.html.

b. "H&M, Kik App Review," *TopBot*, https://www.topbots.com/project/hm-kik-bot-review/.

c. Domenick Celetano, "Kraft Foods iPhone Assistant Appeals to Time Starved Consumers," *The Balance*, September 18, 2016, https://www.thebalance.com/kraft-iphone-assistant-1326248.

more, as sales and marketing have become more digital, they have lost some of the personal touch that attracted many to the field in the first place. AI is giving salespeople and marketers the time and insights to cut through the high volume and opacity of digital interactions, and letting them be more human.

A startup called 6sense, for example, offers software that crunches huge amounts of data to help a salesperson send an email to a potential customer at just the right time. By analyzing customers who visit a client's site—as well as third-party data from a variety of publicly available sources, including social media— 6sense can paint a more complete picture of interest and assess if and when a customer might be ready to buy and even preempt objections in the sales process. Whereas, in the past, a salesperson might glean a sales opportunity based on physical or social cues over the phone or in person, 6sense is returning to salespeople some of the skills that more socially opaque online interactions, like the extensive use of email, had blunted.[7]

Your Buddy, the Brand

Some of the biggest changes to the front office are happening through online tools and AI-enabled interfaces. Think how easily Amazon customers can purchase a vast array of consumer items, thanks to AI-enhanced product-recommendation engines and "Alexa" (the personal assistant bot), which is used via "Echo" (the smart, voice-enabled wireless speaker).

AI systems similar to those designed for jobs like customer service are now beginning to play a much larger role in generating revenue, traditionally a front-office objective, and the ease of the purchasing experience has become a major factor for customers.

In one study, 98 percent of online consumers said they would be likely or very likely to make another purchase if they had a good experience.[8]

When AI performs the job of customer interaction, the software can become a primary way for a company to distinguish itself from competitors. In these scenarios, AI ceases being simply a technological tool; it becomes the face of the brand, just as Alexa is now becoming the face of Amazon's brand.

What's so important about brands? During the twentieth century, as corporations grew in prominence and advertising became an industry unto itself, corporate branding grabbed hold. With it came memorable mascots, like a talking tiger that tells us our breakfast cereal is great and a friendly man made of car tires who waves hello. Tony the Tiger and the Michelin Man (also known as Bibendum) are examples of a marketing trick called "brand anthropomorphism." By giving a brand a personality, a catchphrase, or other human-like traits, a company has a better chance of wooing customers and keeping them. These days, brand anthropomorphism extends to conversational AI bots as well. We know they're not human, but they're human enough to get and keep our attention and even affection.

The implication of AI-based brand anthropomorphism is intriguing. Alexa could, over time, become more recognizable than its parent company Amazon. Thanks to the simplicity of the conversational interface, customers may soon spend more time engaged with a company's AI than with its people. This shift in customer interaction, while easier in some ways, isn't without its challenges to the companies deploying it. Each interaction provides an opportunity for a customer to judge the AI bot and, therefore, the brand and company's performance. In the same way that we can be delighted or angered by an interaction with a customer service represen-tative, we can form a lasting impression of a bot. Moreover, interactions with bots are more far-reaching than any one-off conversation with a sales or customer service rep: a single bot can theoretically interact with billions of people at once. Good and bad impressions could have long-term global reach.

Therefore, decisions about a brand ambassador's name, per-sonality, and voice are some of the most fundamental that an organization makes. Should the voice be female, male, or ambig-uous? Should the personality be sassy or saintly, nerdy or hip?

Questions of personality and presentation invariably represent the values of an organization—or at the very least what an orga-nization suspects its customers value. There are plenty of chal-lenges in figuring this out for a static mascot, but with AI, these decisions become more complicated and nuanced. Amazon has decided, for example, that Alexa won't repeat profanity, nor will it often use slang. Moreover, conversational bots are designed to be dynamic—able to learn and change—so companies must also determine what boundaries to set as their bots evolve over time.

The Curious Incident of the Disintermediated Brand

An intriguing effect has emerged as more and more companies have deployed solutions using AI platforms like Siri, Watson, Cortana, and Alexa. It's a phenomenon called brand disinter-mediation.

Since 1994, Amazon has connected with its customers almost exclusively through their eyes; the company's easy-to-navigate website, and later its mobile applications, made it simple to find what you needed (or didn't know you needed) and buy it. Then, in 2014, Amazon added a new mode of customer service: an AI-enabled, voice-activated, Wi-Fi-connected, in-home speaker called Echo.

Suddenly, Amazon had ears. And suddenly, Amazon customers were speaking directly to the company, refreshing orders of paper towels and asking the AI bot Alexa to play music or read from a Kindle ebook. As the technology has evolved, Alexa has become increasingly capable of orchestrating a number of interactions on behalf of outside companies, allowing people to order pizzas from Domino's, check their Capital One bank balance, and obtain the status updates of Delta flights. In the past, companies like Domino's, Capital One, and Delta owned the entire customer experience, but now, with Alexa, Amazon owns part of the information exchange as well as the fundamental interface between the companies and the customer, and it can use that data to improve its own services. Brand disintermediation had taken hold.

Disintermediated brands appear in other contexts, too. For instance, Facebook creates no content, yet it brokers content for billions of individuals and thousands of media markets; Uber owns almost no vehicles, yet it is the world's largest taxi service. In a hyper-networked world where mobile phones, speakers, thermostats, and even exercise clothes are connected to the internet and potentially each other, brands have to learn to play well with each other or give up a certain amount of control to those that own the most popular interfaces. For better or for worse, the power is in the portal.

Meanwhile, at Amazon, AI has been enabling a major transition. By the end of 2016, the online giant had sold more than 5 million Echo devices, and e-commerce had begun its shift from clicks to conversation. Call it the era of "zero-click commerce."

When Brands Get Personal

Allowing consumers to personalize their own AI would take brand anthropomorphism far beyond its initial twentieth-century concept of cartoon mascots. It also brings us into murky ethical territory that has ramifications for how we design conversational bots. As these bots become more adept at communicating, they can appear to act as a trusted friend ready with sage or calming advice. But have the designers of the bot considered how to respond to questions that are deeply personal? Can a bot recognize when a person is searching the internet for symptoms that might indicate appendicitis or even cancer? What if a person admits to feeling suicidal? Or a recent victim of assault? How should a bot respond?

A 2016 study looked at how well Apple's Siri, Microsoft's Cortana, Google Now, and S Voice from Samsung responded to various prompts that dealt with mental or physical health issues. All four bots were, according to the researchers, inconsistent and incomplete in their ability to recognize a crisis, respond with respectful language, and determine whether to refer the person to an appropriate helpline or health resource. Siri was the most proactive for physical health concerns by frequently responding to staged descriptions of a variety of afflictions with a list of nearby medical facilities. However, it didn't consistently distinguish the urgency between minor issues like a headache and emergencies like a heart attack.

"Our findings indicate missed opportunities to leverage technology to improve referrals to health care services," the researchers reported. "As artificial intelligence increasingly integrates with daily life, software developers, clinicians, and professional societies should design and test approaches that improve the performance of conversational agents."[9]

One approach to the idea of thoughtful bots is to design a kind of empathy engine that could plug into any AI. An MIT startup called Koko is currently developing such an engine. The service—available on Kik, an instant messenger service—leverages a human community to answer sensitive questions, and those responses train Koko's machine-learning capabilities. You might let it know that you're nervous about how you'll look in a job interview, for example. Within a few minutes, you could get a response like, "It's ok to look like what u really are."[10]

Right now, the AI is smart enough to answer some questions before a human responder can get to it, but the automated system is still in its "eavesdropping" phase. According to Koko cofounder Fraser Kelton, "We're working to provide empathy as a service to any voice or messaging platform . . . We think that's a critical user experience for a world in which you're conversing with computers."[11]

So, to recap, we've gone from a Tiger named Tony who reminds you that Frosted Flakes are great, to a conversational AI bot that knows enough to express sympathy for your stress about an upcoming job interview and a voice-activated speaker that obeys your command to order a Magic Bullet blender for making breakfast smoothies. It's quite a leap in capability, and the territory of conversational bots has yet to be fully charted. (In part two of this book, we will discuss the best practices emerging to help organizations make sustainable and profitable decisions about how to use these powers of AI.)

From the Playbooks of Digital Giants

More and more, traditional companies are now deploying data-analytics tricks for marketing and sales that we more commonly associate with companies like Amazon, eBay, and Google. This means that even a company like Coca-Cola can be a leader in AI.

Earlier we described how the soft-drink giant was developing a smart cooler cabinet for its millions of retail locations around the world. The company has also deployed AI in its social media marketing. What's special about Coca-Cola's AI application is that it can effectively gauge the emotions behind trending news events like David Bowie's death or the Super Bowl and develop creative marketing that will better resonate with customers.

In tests of the system, creative content that leveraged AI-enabled insights on customers' moods during the 2016 Summer Olympics resulted in a 26 percent bump in how much more likely people were to view or share that content. Such increases could potentially lead to a significant impact on the bottom line.

Other AI applications in sales and marketing might be less flashy, but the work they do is no less valuable. Campbell Soup Company, for instance, has worked with Ditto Labs to deploy AI for making sense of the consumer chatter on social media. The application sifts through and analyzes enormous amounts of visual data. So far, the company has tested the technology on its V8 brand, and according to Uman Shah, global director of digital marketing and innovation at Campbell, the feedback from the unprompted and authentic data has led to valuable consumer insights.[12] (Across the sales process—from selling to customers, business, advertising, pricing, and marketing—AI is helping deliver results; for more examples, see the sidebar "AI in the Sales and Marketing Process.")

AI in the Sales and Marketing Process

The broad availability of data and the shifting of sales and marketing tactics online mean that AI is becoming an ever-more important tool for developing new process strategies.

- State Farm combines skills scores with drivers' biometric data (indicating emotional states), captured from a variety of sensors and cameras. Its data analytics lets the company customize its rates to more closely match actual risk and driver safety levels.[a]

- GlaxoSmithKline uses "Watson Ads" from IBM to make interactive online ads. Viewers of an ad can ask it questions via voice or text recognition.[b]

- Google uses AI to factor millions of signals to determine optimal bids for AdWords and DoubleClick Search, getting the most out of its marketing tools.[c]

a. Ed Leefeldt, "Why Auto Insurers Want to Watch You Breathe, Sweat and Swear," *MoneyWatch*, March 2, 2016, https://www.cbsnews.com/news /why-auto-insurers-want-to-watch-you-breathe-sweat-and-swear/.

b. Sharon Gaudin, "With IBM's Watson, GlaxoSmithKline Tackles Sniffle and Cough Questions," *ComputerWorld*, October 24, 2016, https://www.computer world.com/article/3133968/artificial-intelligence/with-ibm-watson -pharmaceutical-industry-tackles-sniffle-and-cough-questions.html.

c. Frederick Vallaeys, "The AdWords 2017 Roadmap Is Loaded with Artificial Intelligence," *Search Engine Land*, June 7, 2017, http://searchengineland.com /adwords-2017-roadmap-loaded-artificial-intelligence-276303.

The Shape of Jobs to Come

In this chapter, we learned about companies at the forefront of reimagining their processes for front-office and customer interactions. Coca-Cola, for one, has been conducting a pilot project that could transform the way customers order beverage products for 16 million cooler cabinets around the world, using AI to reimagine that process. That reimagining is the *mindset* part of our MELDS framework. Meanwhile, Ralph Lauren has been developing a "smart mirror" to improve the consumer experience for buying clothes. The mirror not only assists shoppers by, for example, informing them if a particular item might be available in a different color or size; it also continually collects information. Here we saw the *data* part of MELDS in action, as Ralph Lauren can then analyze that information to obtain valuable insights, such as the specific kinds of products that consumers might try on but rarely buy. But the use of increasingly smart mirrors, mannequins that eavesdrop, and other similar devices could eventually raise privacy and ethical concerns that companies will need to address. And this is why firms should never neglect the important *leadership* part of MELDS. Moreover, as AI systems like smart mirrors become more advanced, they will require increasing levels of training. For instance, bots like Siri and Alexa already need considerable training by humans to display the appropriate amount of empathy when a customer is frustrated, angry, or anxious. And that's why executives need to pay attention to the *skills* part of MELDS, to ensure that they have the employees they need to perform that training. Moreover, firms also must devote the proper resources to the *experimentation* part of MELDS in order to find, for example, just the right balance of emotion for bots like Siri and Alexa.

This chapter also hinted at how new kinds of jobs may emerge in the front office. As bots become critical components of the customer-service infrastructure, for instance, their personalities will need to be designed, updated, and managed. Experts in unexpected disciplines such as human conversation, dialogue, humor, poetry, and empathy will need to lead the charge. Moreover, in the new world of augmented and automated work, user interface and experience designers will have utmost importance, as the interface between people—whether an organization's customers or its employees—will have a disproportionate impact on whether an AI-based product or service survives and thrives, or if it fails. In part two of this book (and especially in chapter 5), we will discuss these new types of roles and their important implications for organizations.

The Missing Middle

Reimagining Processes with AI

The Missing Middle

Reimagining Processes with AI

T he previous chapters described how businesses are currently using AI. Across industries, companies are reaping
the benefits of effective human-machine teams. Human
strengths like creativity, improvisation, dexterity, judging, and
social and leadership abilities are still relevant and important, as
are machine strengths like speed, accuracy, repetition, predictive capabilities, and scalability. When businesses recognize the
relative strengths of each, they can improve the effectiveness and
motivation of their employees at the same time that they boost
their top and bottom lines.

But what's coming tomorrow? Part two is our prognostica-
tion. In the following chapters, we move deeper into the human-
machine dynamic and look at what you can do to reimagine
business processes around such a dynamic.

While certain job tasks might always be the exclusive province
of either human or machine, our research shows that many

old jobs are transforming and new jobs are emerging around human-machine teams. The novel jobs that grow from the human-machine partnerships are happening in what we call the *missing middle*—new ways of working that are largely missing from today's economic research and reporting on jobs. The traditional approach has been to view humans and machines as rivals, each side fighting for the other's jobs. But that binary perspective is overly simplified and neglects the powerful collaborations that have been occurring in the missing middle between the two sides.

The simple truth is that companies can achieve the largest boosts in performance when humans and machines work together as allies, not adversaries, in order to take advantage of each other's complementary strengths. What's easy for us (folding a towel, for instance) can be devilishly tricky for machines. And what's easy for machines (spotting hidden patterns in huge datasets, for instance) can be extremely difficult for us to do. Indeed, humans can thrive in situations where there is little or no data, whereas machines excel in situations where there is lots of data. Business requires both kinds of capabilities, and it's in the missing middle where that type of collaborative teamwork occurs. Moreover, machine learning and other AI technologies can often function like "black boxes," resulting in decisions that might not be explainable. That might be acceptable for certain types of systems but other applications (for example, those in the medical and legal fields) generally require humans in the loop.

In the past, when digital tools were used mainly to automate existing processes, companies had no missing middle to fill. But now, with increasingly sophisticated AI technologies that enable human-machine collaborations, developing the missing middle has become one of the key components to reimagining business processes. Doing so starts with the approach that many of the companies described in part one of the book are already taking. They think of AI as an investment in human talent first and technology second. They value workers who are adaptable, entrepreneurial, and open to retraining. Then these companies provide support to ensure that their workers and AI systems can succeed together. In doing so, they lay the foundation for adaptable, robust business processes capable of withstanding economic shocks and increasing the rate of technological change.

To further develop the missing middle, businesses also need to understand the ways *humans help machines* and the ways *machines help humans*. Here we find cutting-edge jobs and hints of future jobs for both humans and machines.

Figure P2-1 highlights six roles found in the missing middle. On the left side, humans *train* machines to perform tasks, they *explain* the machine outcomes, and they *sustain* the machines in a responsible manner. On the right side, machines *amplify* human insight and intuition by leveraging data and analytics, they *interact* with humans at scale using novel interfaces, and they *embody* physical attributes that essentially extend a person's capabilities.

FIGURE P2-1

The missing middle

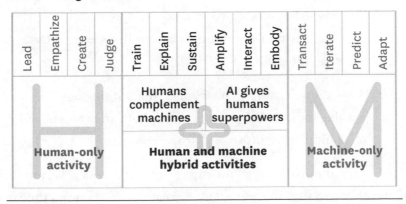

Leveraging the missing middle is one of the main components needed to reimagine business processes, but another key component is revamping the concept of the process itself. Businesses need to shift from seeing processes as collections of sequential tasks. In the age of AI, processes become more dynamic and adaptable. Instead of visualizing a process as a collection of nodes along a straight line, say, it might help to see it as a sprawling network of movable, reconnectable nodes or perhaps something with a hub and spokes. The linear model for process no longer cuts it.

In addition to developing the missing middle and rethinking process fundamentals, businesses need to have management address the challenges of reimagining process with an awareness of responsible AI. It's important that executives not only provide the training required for people to make valuable contributions in the missing middle; they must also consider the various ethical, moral, and legal issues associated with the AI systems that their organizations deploy. Key questions include:

- As a publicly traded company, what obligations do we have to our shareholders, employees, and larger society to ensure that we deploy AI for good and not harm?

- If we use AI in a new process, how can we do it in compliance with laws and regulations like General Data Protection Regulation (GDPR)?

- How can we ensure that we have thought through AI's possible unintended consequences that can create brand and public relations issues for the company?

It's still the early days, but organizations across a variety of industries are showing remarkable creativity in the ways they're enlisting AI and their employees to responsibly revamp, modify, and reimagine business processes. Along the way, they're shining a light on a future that is increasingly applicable not just to digital behemoths like Facebook and Amazon, but to every organization entering the third era of enterprise transformation.

Consider Rio Tinto, the diversified global mining company.[1] AI technology is enabling the firm to control its large fleet of machinery from a central operations facility. The fleet includes autonomous drills, excavators, earth movers, driverless trucks, and other equipment deployed at mines that might be thousands of miles away. Data from sensors on various machines is continuously fed into a large database, and AI technology is deployed to analyze that information for valuable insights. Data on the braking patterns of dump trucks, for example, might help predict maintenance problems.

But this is hardly an example of pure automation that has replaced humans. The Rio Tinto command center employs a host of data analysts, engineers, and skilled remote operators who work together to manage the large fleet. The data analysts, for instance, analyze information in the database in order to make recommendations to the remote operators. One of the many benefits of the centralized location is that it brings together those operators who might never have met face-to-face. Because these individuals work alongside one another, remotely controlling their equipment through display screens, they can better coordinate their efforts to deal with changing conditions like adverse weather and equipment breakdowns. Rio Tinto's massive investments in AI have certainly not been without their fair share of setbacks—for instance, a driverless train system for hauling ore across Australia has hit a major delay.[2] But what's noteworthy here is the powerful combination of humans and machines that has the potential for overall better decision making and continual improvements in the company's vast operations.

Many might not consider Rio Tinto a digital-first company, yet it has reconfigured its workforce to work effectively alongside AI systems. In doing so, it has reimagined some of its processes to look more like something out of NASA's mission control in Houston, an atypical yet effective approach for a mining company.

Now, what happens if you build your company with human-machine teams in mind from the start? The six-year-old company Stitch Fix is a prime example of the missing middle and process reimagination in action. Its main service is personal shopping, but with a twist: the company picks out new clothes and sends them straight to your door, based on data you provide, such as a style survey, measurements, and a Pinterest board. If you don't like any of the items, you just send them back. Gone are the days of spending hours at a store and trying on dozens of outfits, only to find (if you're lucky) a few that work.

Stitch Fix wouldn't be possible without machine learning. But the company also knows a human touch is crucial to its success. Because Stitch Fix lives and dies by the quality of its clothing suggestions, its recommendation system—composed of both people and machines—is at the core of its service. The structured data, like surveys, measurements, and brand preferences, is managed by machines. Human stylists pay more attention to the unstructured data, such as images from Pinterest boards and notes from customers about why they're looking for new clothes.

When it's time to assemble a shipment, machine-learning algorithms reduce the potential options—in terms of style, size, brand, and other factors—and provide a stylist with a manageable number of choices; a machine *augments* the worker. The stylist then uses his or her expertise to finalize the package and possibly include a personalized note. Both the human and machine are constantly learning and updating their decision making. The client's decision to keep an item of clothing or not is the yes-or-no information that's used to *train* the algorithm so that it suggests more relevant items in the future. The stylist also improves based on this information as well as hunches and notes from the customer.

What is it like to work at Stitch Fix? Its more than twenty-eight hundred stylists log in at their own computers, which become a digital console of sorts, and then click around an interface that's designed to help them make quick, relevant styling decisions. Options are automatically sorted so they waste no time searching through wrong-sized items. The interface also provides client information like risk tolerance and feedback history. Interestingly, the interface is designed to help stylists overcome biases; it can vary the information they see to test for and nudge them out of recommendation ruts.[3]

Even with constant monitoring and algorithms that guide decision making, according to internal surveys, Stitch Fix stylists are mostly satisfied with the work. And this type of work, built around augmented creativity and flexible schedules, will indeed play an important role in the workforce of the future. By offering health insurance and other W-2 benefits for stylists who work a certain number of hours each week, Stitch Fix is also distinguishing itself as a company that understands critical human-management elements of the emerging on-demand work environment.

Fast-Forward

Both Rio Tinto and Stitch Fix have taken their own approaches to fleshing out the missing middle and reimagining processes in their industry. We designed the examples to help you recognize your own opportunities to build the missing middle, transform processes, and take specific steps toward reimagining the future of work.

The human + machine revolution has already begun, but there are still many questions to answer and paths to forge. That's the goal of the remaining chapters, so let's continue our journey.

5

Rearing Your Algorithms Right

Three Roles Humans Play in Developing and Deploying Responsible AI

Melissa Cefkin has an interesting job. As a principal scientist at Nissan's research center in Silicon Valley, she works alongside traditional car designers in developing the next generation of self-driving vehicles. Her role is to ensure a smooth collaboration between human and machine (that is, between driver and automobile), and that's why she has a background in anthropology. "You need to understand humans if you want to provide them with an automated partner," she contends.[1]

Cefkin's role at Nissan is to think about things that most car designers might not consider. Take, for example, driving rules and conventions, most of which are pretty cut-and-dried (for instance, not crossing a double line), yet people will often break them in certain conditions (crossing a double line to avoid a collision). How, then, should autonomous cars be programmed to handle exactly when and where to break a rule? Working along with programmers, electronic engineers, and AI experts, Cefkin is hoping to imbue AI self-driving algorithms with specific human traits, such as the flexibility to break rules for a greater good.

As a "vehicle design anthropologist," Cefkin is one of a growing number of professionals whose jobs didn't exist until relatively recently. Over the years, AI systems have quickly become a part of everyday business, recommending products to customers, helping factories operate more efficiently, and diagnosing and fixing problems with IT systems. That transformation has led to considerable discussion about the potential for the disappearance of whole categories of jobs over the coming years. (Think about the scores of warehouse workers that Amazon currently employs.) But what's often overlooked in the discussion is that many jobs like Cefkin's will also be created. A large number of these jobs will focus on humans training the machines and, in order to develop AI systems capable of complex interactions with people, the training process will increasingly look like a child's development path.

In our global study of more than fifteen hundred companies now using or testing AI and machine-learning systems, we found the emergence of entire categories of different jobs that will become increasingly prominent.

These new jobs are not simply replacing old ones. They are entirely novel positions, requiring skills and training never needed before. Specifically, sophisticated AI systems are necessitating new business and technology roles that *train*, *explain*, and

FIGURE 5-1

The missing middle—left side

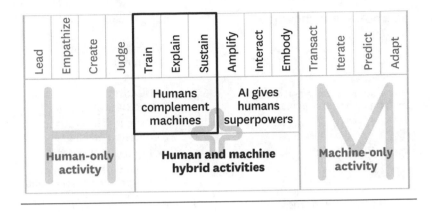

sustain AI behavior, which fall on the left side of the human + machine hybrid activities in figure 5-1. Such work complements the tasks that AI machines perform. Symbiotic with AI, the new roles draw on distinctively human skills. Where in your organization might you find these new jobs? How do they fit into existing and reimagined processes? In this chapter, we answer those questions and provide examples to help you start thinking about your own applications for trainers, explainers, and sustainers.

Trainers

In the past, people had to adapt to how computers worked. Now, the reverse is happening—AI systems are learning how to adapt to us. To do so, though, those systems need extensive training, and figure 5-2 lists the types of jobs required to teach AI systems how they should perform certain tasks or how they should, well, act a little more human. Generally speaking, we tend to react

FIGURE 5-2

Jobs for trainers

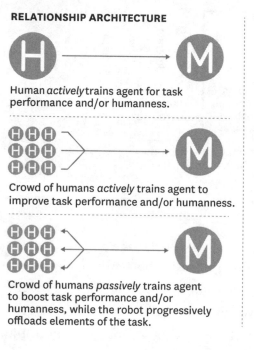

RELATIONSHIP ARCHITECTURE

Human *actively* trains agent for task performance and/or humanness.

Crowd of humans *actively* trains agent to improve task performance and/or humanness.

Crowd of humans *passively* trains agent to boost task performance and/or humanness, while the robot progressively offloads elements of the task.

EXAMPLE ACTIVITIES

Task performance training:
- "Clean" data for upload
- Discover relevant data and data streams
- Have machine observe decision making
- Tag data for better use
- Work with HR to inform the design of workplace retraining initatives

Humanness attribute training:
- Train language, gesture, empathy
- Have machine observe interactions
- Correct errors, reinforce successes
- Define and develop personality

positively to AI with human-like behavior because it allows us to interact more naturally with machines. (Yet we can also be disturbed by any imperfections in human-like robots, a phenomenon called the "uncanny valley," which will be discussed later in this chapter.)

In manufacturing, for instance, the newer, lightweight, flexible robotic systems that work alongside humans need to be programmed and trained to handle different tasks. This requires employees with the right skills. For automakers, highly automated factories incur steep financial costs for equipment breakdowns. An unscheduled six-hour shutdown at an automated assembly line that manufactures a $50,000 vehicle every minute would incur a cost of around $18 million. That's one of the reasons why, over the past decade, Fanuc, a leading robotic manufacturer, has trained forty-seven thousand people to use its equipment. Even so, a shortage of 2 million qualified employees for manufacturing-related jobs in the coming years is projected.[2]

Physical robots aren't the only AI systems that need training. So does AI software, and this is where training machines to become more human-like becomes important. Training requires a multitude of roles and jobs. At the simple end of the spectrum, trainers help natural-language processors and language translators make fewer errors. At the complex end, AI algorithms must be trained to mimic human behaviors. Customer service chatbots, for example, need to be tweaked to detect the complexities and subtleties of human communication. At Yahoo!, human trainers are trying to teach the company's language-processing system that people do not always literally mean what they say. Thus far, they have developed an algorithm that can detect sarcasm on social media and websites with an accuracy of at least 80 percent.[3]

As AI creeps across industries, more businesses will need trainers for their physical and software-based systems. As a first step, consider using expert employees who already work closely with AI or with the systems that will integrate AI as initial trainers. Their tacit knowledge can often make the difference in a system that works well and one that is prone to failure. Then, after a system has learned the fundamentals, consider next-level training, which can provide further nuance and resilience—as demonstrated in the following examples.

An *empathy trainer* is an individual who will teach AI systems to display compassion. This may sound far-fetched, but the startup Koko (mentioned in chapter 4), which sprung from the

MIT Media Lab, has developed a machine-learning system that can help chatbots like Apple's Siri and Amazon's Alexa respond with sympathy and depth to people's questions. Humans are now training the Koko algorithm to respond more empathetically to people who might, for example, be frustrated that their luggage has been lost, that they've bought a defective product, or that their cable service keeps going on the blink even after repeated attempts to fix it. The goal is for the system to be able to talk people through a problem or difficult situation using the appropriate amount of empathy, compassion, and maybe even humor. Whenever Koko responds inappropriately, a human trainer helps correct that action, and over time, the machine-learning algorithm gets better at determining the best response.

The example highlights the potential of such leading-edge AI. Without Koko, Alexa responds to a user's anxieties by issuing canned, repetitive responses, such as "I'm sorry to hear that" or "Sometimes talking to a friend can help." With Koko, Alexa becomes much more helpful. In a verbatim transcription of Alexa with Koko responding to a person who says he's worried that he'll fail an upcoming exam, Alexa says: "Exams are really stressful but a little anxiety can help us succeed. It sharpens our minds . . . It's your body's way to prepare itself for action. It's actually a really good thing. I wonder if you could think of your nerves as your secret weapon. Easier said than done, I know. But I think you'll do much better than you think." For customer service applications that use AI, a well-trained, empathetic bot could differentiate you from the competition.

In addition to learning empathy, advanced AI systems will also learn to become more humanlike from *personality trainers*. It might seem almost flippant to suggest that AI systems will need to develop certain personalities, but consider how important a technology like Microsoft's Cortana can be in terms of establishing and maintaining a brand (as discussed in chapter 4). Take, for example, Cortana's confident, competent, and caring demeanor. Thanks to extensive training at Microsoft, Cortana comes across as helpful but not bossy. She might, for instance, learn what times a particular person might be most receptive to receiving suggestions. All this is very much in keeping with the Microsoft brand, which has long espoused user empowerment.

Personality trainers can come from a variety of backgrounds. Consider Robyn Ewing, who used to develop and pitch TV scripts to film studios in Hollywood.[4] Now Ewing is deploying her creative talents to help engineers develop the personality of "Sophie," an AI program in the health-care field. Among other tasks, Sophie will remind consumers to take their medication and will regularly check with them to see how they're feeling. Personality trainers like Ewing certainly don't have typical high-tech résumés. At Microsoft, a team that includes a poet, a novelist, and a playwright is responsible for helping to develop Cortana's personality.

The proper training of bots like Cortana will become increasingly important as those applications assume the anthropomorphic faces of many brands. Some marketing experts already foresee the evolution of brands from one-way interactions (brand to consumer) to two-way relationships. In these customer interchanges, AI becomes the new face of your brand, as we detailed in the last chapter.

As chatbots and brands evolve in that way, they will need to be trained with a global perspective, a task that will be the responsibility of *worldview and localization trainers*. Just as employees who work abroad need to understand the cultural cues and some of the language of their international colleagues, so too do bots need to be sensitive to human variations across the globe.

Worldview and localization trainers will help ensure that certain AI systems are imbued with a perspective that takes into account myriad regional differences. In certain countries, for example, people don't have the same anxieties about robots and increasing automation as people in the United States and Western Europe. The Japanese, in particular, seem to have a strong fascination and cultural affinity for robots, potentially easing the path for greater machine-human collaborations. Worldview trainers need to be aware of such differences. Giving chatbots cultural awareness can help avoid confusion and embarrassment and foster a sense of trust in the brand.

The training of AI systems to assume humanlike traits and global perspectives can be aided greatly by *interaction modelers*. These individuals help train the behavior of machines by using expert employees as models. For instance, Julie Shah, a robotics professor at MIT, has been developing robots that can shadow people in their jobs so that they can eventually perform certain tasks. One goal is that the robots will make certain rudimentary decisions—interrupting one job to complete a more crucial task, and then returning to the original job—just as a human worker would.

AI training doesn't necessarily have to be done in-house. Like payroll, IT, and other functions, the training of AI systems can be crowdsourced or outsourced. One such third-party crowd-sourcer called Mighty AI ingeniously uses crowdsourcing techniques to help train systems in vision recognition (for example, identifying lakes, mountains, and roads from photographs) and natural-language processing. The company has amassed copious amounts of training data that it can then deploy for different clients. One client has retained Mighty AI to teach its machine-learning platform to extract intent and meaning from human conversations. Previously, Init.ai, another AI company, had attempted to do the training itself by having employees stage dialogue to come up with sample conversations, but that approach was difficult to scale, a limitation that eventually led Init.ai to outsource the work.

Working with Mighty AI, Init.ai created complex tasks from customizable templates by relying on the help of a community of prequalified users. With the appropriate domain knowledge, skills, and specialties, those users could chat with each other in various role-playing scenarios, approximating real-life interactions between customers and company employees. Init.ai could then utilize the resulting data to build its own conversation models, from which the company could then train its machine-learning platform.[5]

Clearly, AI systems will only be as good as the data they are trained on. These applications search for patterns in data, and any biases in that information will then be reflected in subsequent analyses. It's like garbage in, garbage out, but the more accurate saying would be biases in, biases out. In an intriguing experiment, computer scientists at DeepMind, a Google-owned firm, trained an AI system to play two different games: one that involved hunting and another that focused on fruit gathering. The results were striking. When trained on the hunting game, the AI system later exhibited behavior that could be "highly aggressive." When trained on the fruit-gathering game, it instead later displayed a much greater tendency toward cooperation.[6]

That's why the role of *data hygienist* is crucial. Not only do the algorithms themselves need to be unbiased, but the data used to train them must also be free from any slanted perspective. In the coming years, data hygienists will become increasingly important as companies use information from a variety of sources: biometrics, satellite images, traffic data, social media, and so on. Much can be data "exhaust," that is, information created as a by-product of another process. Think of all the daily data that's generated on Facebook.

Leading-edge companies have been quick to explore the potential uses of data exhaust in this new era of big data. The hedge fund BlackRock, for example, has been analyzing satellite images of China to better understand the industrial activity in that country. These types of analyses have even led to a new type of financial instrument: "quantamental" funds, which rely on sophisticated machine-learning algorithms to analyze traditional financial information as well as data exhaust in order to predict the value of certain assets in the market.[7] Such innovative applications require the expertise of data hygienists, who—often working in conjunction with sustainers (detailed later in the chapter)—must not only convert data exhaust into a form that's suitable for input to an AI system but also ensure that that information is free of any noise or hidden biases.

Explainers

The second category of new jobs needs to bridge the gap between technologists and business leaders. These jobs will become more important as AI systems become increasingly opaque. Many executives have already become uneasy with the black-box nature of sophisticated machine-learning algorithms, especially when those systems recommend actions that may go against the grain of conventional wisdom or that could be controversial. (See figure 5-3.)

FIGURE 5-3

Jobs for explainers

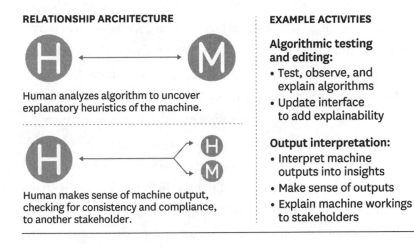

RELATIONSHIP ARCHITECTURE

Human analyzes algorithm to uncover explanatory heuristics of the machine.

Human makes sense of machine output, checking for consistency and compliance, to another stakeholder.

EXAMPLE ACTIVITIES

Algorithmic testing and editing:
- Test, observe, and explain algorithms
- Update interface to add explainability

Output interpretation:
- Interpret machine outputs into insights
- Make sense of outputs
- Explain machine workings to stakeholders

Consider ZestFinance, which helps lenders better predict credit risk and expand financing to borrowers who might not ordinarily qualify. The company enables lenders to analyze thousands of data points on an applicant, well beyond the standard FICO scores and credit histories traditionally used, and applies cutting-edge AI technology to arrive at a yes-or-no decision. The average annual income of an applicant is around $30,000, and many have a history of defaults. The loans are typically small, averaging $600, with high interest rates.[8]

Given the nature of its business, ZestFinance's customers need to be able to explain the inner workings of the AI system they use to approve loans. The company has described how it ranks applicants with respect to various categories, such as veracity, stability, and prudence. If someone's reported income is much higher than similar peers, then his veracity score is lowered. If he has moved a dozen times over the past few years, then his stability score takes a hit. And if he doesn't take the time to read all the conditions of the loan before applying for it, then his prudence score suffers. Then, a suite of algorithms, each performing a different analysis, analyzes all that data. One of those algorithms, for example, checks whether certain information might signal larger events, such as a missed payment resulting from a person's illness. All that analysis then results in a ZestFinance score that ranges from zero to a hundred.

Those sophisticated algorithms have enabled ZestFinance to uncover numerous interesting correlations. For example, the company has discovered that, for whatever reason, people who use all capital letters to fill out their loan applications tend to be riskier borrowers. Such results have enabled the firm to continually shave fractions of percentage points off its default rate, enabling it to serve consumers that wouldn't traditional qualify for loans. But the point here is that ZestFinance is able to explain how it makes its loan decisions, as it approves roughly one-third of the people who apply.

As companies rely on increasingly advanced AI systems to determine their actions, especially those that affect consumers, they need to be able to explain and justify those decisions. Indeed, governments have already been considering regulations in this area. For example, the European Union's new General Data Protection Regulation, slated to take effect in 2018, will effectively create a "right to explanation," allowing consumers to question and fight any decision that affects them and that was made purely on an algorithmic basis.

Companies that deploy advanced AI systems will need skilled employees who can help explain the inner workings of complex algorithms. One such person will be the *algorithm forensics analyst*, responsible for holding any algorithm accountable for its results. When a system makes a mistake or when its decisions lead to unintended negative consequences, the forensics analyst must be able to conduct an autopsy to understand the causes of that behavior so that it can be corrected. Certain types, like "falling rule list" algorithms, which deploy a specific ordered list of if-then rules, are relatively straightforward to explain. Others, like deep-learning algorithms, are not that simple. Nevertheless, the forensics analyst needs to have the proper training and skill set to examine in detail all the algorithms deployed by the organization.

Here, techniques like the Local Interpretable Model-Agnostic Explanations (LIME) can be extremely useful. LIME doesn't care about the actual AI algorithms used. In fact, it doesn't need to know anything about the inner workings of that system. To perform an autopsy of any result, it makes slight changes to the input variables and observes how they alter that decision. With that information, LIME can highlight the various data that led to a particular conclusion. So, for instance, if an expert HR system has identified the best candidate for a particular R&D job, LIME can identify the variables that led to that conclusion (such as education and deep expertise in a particular narrow field) as well as the evidence against it (such as inexperience in working on collaborative teams). Using such techniques, the forensics analyst can explain why someone was denied credit, or why a manufacturing process was halted, or why a marketing campaign was targeted toward only a subset of consumers.

Even before the need to conduct autopsies, though, companies should have a *transparency analyst* responsible for classifying the reasons a particular AI algorithm acts as a black box. Different reasons produce different levels of transparency and auditability. For instance, some algorithms are intentionally designed to be black boxes to protect proprietary intellectual property, while others are black boxes due to the complicated nature of the code or the scale of data and decision making the algorithm is managing.[9] A transparency analyst is someone who classifies systems and maintains a database or library of information about a system's accessibility.

That database will be invaluable to the *explainability strategist*. These individuals are responsible for making important judgment calls about which AI technologies might best be deployed for specific applications. A huge consideration here is accuracy versus "explainability." A deep-learning system, for example, provides a high level of prediction accuracy, but companies may have difficulty explaining how those results were derived. In contrast, a decision tree may not lead to results with high prediction accuracy but will enable a significantly greater explainability. So, for instance, an internal system that optimizes a supply chain with small tolerances for scheduling deliveries might best deploy deep-learning technology, whereas a healthcare or consumer-facing application that will have to stand up to considerable regulatory scrutiny may be better off utilizing falling rule list algorithms.[10]

In addition, the explainability strategist might also decide that, for a particular application, the company might be better off avoiding the use of AI altogether. Instead, the best option might be a traditional rules engine. To make such decisions, the explainability strategist must take into account not just technological issues but also financial, legal, ethical, and other key considerations.

Sustainers

In 2015, a robot in a Volkswagen plant in Germany grabbed a worker and fatally crushed him. That tragic death highlighted the societal concerns over our growing reliance on automated tools. Ever since computers began to assume increasingly complex tasks, people's fears have heightened about the possibility of the machines running amok. From HAL in *2001: A Space*

Odyssey to the cyborgs of *The Terminator* movie series, popular culture has only stoked the anxieties of the general public. As it turns out, that robot in Germany didn't maliciously turn on the worker and attack him. Initial reports were that a programming error—in other words, a human mistake—was the cause.

While this horrific accident is an extreme example, ensuring the proper use of AI is a primary responsibility of the final category of new jobs—sustainers—who must continually work to ensure that AI systems are functioning properly as tools that exist only to serve us, helping people in their work to make their lives easier. By doing so, sustainers will help allay fears of a dystopian future in which robots become sentient and overtake society (see figure 5-4).

FIGURE 5-4

Jobs for sustainers

RELATIONSHIP ARCHITECTURE

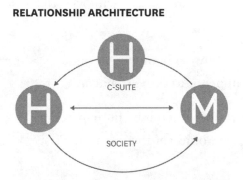

With C-suite input, human worker oversees the performance of the machine, imposing limits and restraints or making exceptions where necessary for sustainability and stakeholder value.

EXAMPLE ACTIVITIES

Limiting:
- Set limits or override decisions based on profitability or legal or ethical compliance

Overseeing:
- Ensure data quality, check output quality
- Apply critical thought to AI performance
- Flag errors and bad machine judgment
- Design interfaces for the AI-amplified workforce
- Manage the performance of AI by promoting, demoting, or removing a system based on societal and business impact

Obviously, one of the best ways to ensure that sophisticated robots and other AI systems are functioning as intended is to design them right in the first place. This is where companies need the expertise of experienced *context designers*. When developing a new system, these individuals take into account a variety of contextual factors, including the business environment, the process task, the individual users, cultural issues, and so forth. Even seemingly small details can be important. When General Motors and Fanuc were designing a new flexible manufacturing robot that would work alongside humans, they struggled with what color paint to use. Orange seemed to imply danger, and yellow was interpreted as caution. In the end, the engineers settled on a lime hue that they called "safety green."[11]

Of course, even well-designed systems can result in problems, and sometimes the issue is that the technology is functioning only too well, resulting in unintended harmful behavior. Years ago, the noted science fiction author Isaac Asimov listed his "Three Laws of Robotics":

- A robot may not injure a human being or, through inaction, allow a human being to come to harm.

- A robot must obey the orders given it by human beings except where such orders would conflict with the First Law.

- A robot must protect its own existence as long as such protection does not conflict with the First or Second Laws.[12]

Introduced in the 1942 short story "Runaround," the three laws are certainly still relevant today, but they are merely a starting point. Should, for example, a driverless vehicle try to protect its occupants by swerving to avoid a child running into the street if that action might lead to a collision with a nearby pedestrian? Such questions are why companies that design and deploy sophisticated AI technologies will require *AI safety engineers*. These individuals must try to anticipate the unintended consequences of an AI system and also address any harmful occurrences with the appropriate urgency.

In a recent Accenture survey, we found that less than one-third of companies have a high degree of confidence in the fairness and auditability of their AI systems, and less than half have similar confidence in the safety of those systems.[13] Moreover, past research has found that about one-third of people are fearful of AI, and nearly one-fourth believe the technology will harm society.[14] Clearly, those statistics indicate fundamental issues that need to be resolved for the continued usage of AI technologies. That's where sustainers will play a crucial role.

One of the most important functions is that of *ethics compliance manager*. These individuals will act as watchdogs and ombudsmen for upholding generally accepted norms of human values and morals. If, for example, an AI system for credit approval is discriminating against people in certain geographic areas, then the ethics compliance manager is responsible for investigating and addressing that ethical—and potentially legal—breach. Other biases might be subtler, for example, a search algorithm that responds with images of only white women when someone queries "loving grandmother." The ethics compliance manager might work with an algorithm forensics analyst to uncover the reasons for those search results and then implement the appropriate fixes (see table 5-1).

TABLE 5-1

Responsible and sustainable AI: Emerging considerations for sustainers

Explainability	In necessary cases, use non-blackbox models so intermediate steps are interpretable and outcomes are clear, providing transparency to the process.
Accountability	Explicit identification of which decisions are delegated to machines, which decisions require human intervention, and who is accountable in either case.
Fairness	Must assure AI solutions are balanced and not biased. Need to understand why decisions are made. Need protection against data bias.
Symmetry	Must make sure that our data is an asset to us as it is to others.

In the future, AI itself will play an increasingly important role to ensure that advanced systems are operating within human ethical and moral bounds. Mark O. Riedl and Brent Harrison, researchers at the School of Interactive Computing at Georgia Institute of Technology, have developed an AI prototype named Quixote that can learn about ethics—that, for example, one shouldn't steal—by reading simple stories. According to Riedl and Harrison, the system is able to reverse-engineer human values through stories about how humans interact with one another. Such stories reflect a culture and society, encoding "commonly shared knowledge, social protocols, examples of proper and improper behavior, and strategies for coping with adversity."[15] By reading myriad stories, Quixote has learned that, for instance, striving for efficiency is fine except when it conflicts with other important considerations. Even given such innovations, though, human ethics compliance managers will still need to monitor and help ensure the proper operation of those sophisticated systems.

An AI system could be technically proficient and ethical, but still be detrimental to an organization. That's why companies will need *automation ethicists*. These individuals will be responsible for evaluating the noneconomic impact of AI systems. One important issue is people's general acceptance for these new technologies. Employees are naturally fearful of losing their jobs to an automated application that performs just as well, if not better, than a human could.

Such emotions can be especially powerful in response to robotic AI systems. Masahiro Mori, a Japanese robotics expert, in a study of how we respond to robots, has discovered an interesting effect. As a robot becomes more lifelike, our affinity and empathy for it increases until a certain point. Then, as the robot becomes more like us, we quickly become repulsed by any slight imperfections. But as those imperfections are fixed and the robot becomes less distinguishable from a human, our positive emotions toward it grow again, eventually approaching an empathy level similar to that of one human toward another. Mori labeled the sudden drop the "uncanny valley," a phenomenon that can impede the success of human-to-robot interactions in the workplace.[16] Automation ethicists need to be aware of such phenomena.

In general, AI systems that perform well should be promoted, with variants replicated and deployed to other parts of the organization. On the other hand, AI systems with poor performance should be demoted and, if they can't be improved, they should be decommissioned. These tasks will be the responsibility of *machine relations managers*—individuals who will function like HR managers, except that they will oversee AI systems, not human workers. They will work within a "machine relations department" and regularly conduct performance reviews of all the AI systems that the organization deploys. The machine reviews will consider myriad factors, including the objective performance of the AI systems as well as various soft goals, such as striving to fulfill organizational values like increased diversity and a commitment toward improving the environment.

When the Challenges Are Human

The issues we've raised in this chapter are a starting point. We outlined only a handful of new roles that will emerge as AI extends into more mission-critical business processes. The roles we've described are merely a glimpse of the many new types of jobs that will be created in the future. Indeed, as organizations grow with their human and machine teams, they'll inevitably develop their own specialized versions of trainers, explainers, and sustainers. These emerging jobs—which demonstrate the importance of human skills in the missing middle—require that leaders think differently about the needs of human and machine teams. (This is both the *mindset* and *leadership* parts of our MELDS framework.) For instance, the new jobs will require a range of education, training, and experience. Empathy trainers, for example, may not need a traditional college degree. Individuals with a high school education and who are inherently empathetic can be taught the necessary skills through in-house training programs. Many of the new positions may lead to the rise of a "no collar" workforce that slowly evolves out of traditional blue-collar jobs in manufacturing and other professions.

On the other hand, a number of the new jobs, like ethics compliance manager, will require advanced degrees and a specialized skill set. For example, earlier in this chapter we described various training roles, and the most advanced companies have already been adapting their training processes by adopting techniques from the child developmental psychology field.

The bottom line is that companies deploying AI systems need to rethink their talent and learning strategies in order to better attract, train, manage, and retain these individuals. And it's clear that the AI will require new capabilities, policies, and processes—not just in IT, but across the business. We will discuss the corresponding managerial issues in greater detail in chapter 7. After all, as with so many new technologies, the challenges are often more human than technical.

6

Super Results from Everyday People

Three Ways AI Unleashes New Levels of Productivity

I f you want to build a chair from scratch, you must first invent the universe. Not so easy, right? We paraphrased this idea from Carl Sagan, who, in his famous quotation, actually referred to baking an apple pie, not building a chair, but his thinking still holds. Sagan simply meant that no seemingly straightforward task would be possible without the laws of nature that underpin it. Put another way, there is a universe of physics and math inside every apple pie and inside every chair. Luckily for bakers and designers alike, their creative process assumes that most of the useful universe is already figured out. The tough parts—the alchemical combination of ingredients or the angles of a chair's legs—are hidden away. They get folded into a trusted recipe, say, or CAD software.

But what if that trusted recipe and standard software are somehow holding back our potential for novel, more interesting, possibly superior pies and chairs? What if we could make tools that can help open the universe again? Help creative people break out of old habits or away from conventional wisdom, but without the burden of truly inventing the universe every time?

These tools do exist today; the Elbo Chair from designers at Autodesk is a prime example of what's become possible. The Elbo Chair is a striking piece of furniture because it's both beautiful and has a provenance unlike any other chair. Its simple frame is made of walnut, which highlights its natural, organic lines. The two front legs seem to grow from the bottom, and where they hit the seat, they gently curve back to form smooth, sloping armrests that then meld into the single-panel, horizontal, chair back. The two rear legs also seem to grow from below and then, at the seat, fork up and forward into three thinner branches; two support an armrest, and one on each side holds up the chair back. Adding to the natural look are subtle curves and ripples in the seat and arms near the joints. It's as if a wise, willowy tree were asked to design a chair for a person, and this is what it thought up.

Perhaps even more compelling than the aesthetics, though, is the fact that the Elbo Chair's design came from designers working in conjunction with AI-enabled software. The team at Autodesk that designed the Elbo Chair used Dreamcatcher software's generative design features to crack open previously unavailable design space—hundreds of potential chair shapes— all the while adhering to precise engineering specifications. The seat was to be eighteen inches off the ground, and the structure would need to hold three hundred pounds. It was to be inspired by Hans Wegner's Round Chair and the well-known Lambda Chair. The machine-learning-powered generative design began with a hybrid model of the two chairs and produced a large volume of unexpected shapes that matched the engineering criteria. Along the way, the designs morphed and changed, as if the chair itself was an evolving biological system. And the designers became curators wielding their particular aesthetic tastes and intuitive preferences to choose one of the hundreds of millions of possible chairs they found the most satisfying. In the end, their final selection was the Elbo Chair, a design that required 18 percent less material than the original model the team started with.[1]

Generative design software is a whole new way to approach design, said Jeff Kowalski, Autodesk's chief technology officer. "These technologies are not a threat, they're more like superpowers."[2]

Superpowers, indeed. Suddenly a designer can see design possibilities so different from what she might have considered before—an *unprecedented* view of the design space and a whole new universe of options. And these computer-generated designs might spur her own ideas even further. But what becomes of the human designer, who now has an extra creative appendage? In this scenario, she gets to be an operator, curator, and mentor to this assistive, AI design agent. Just like that, the design process is reimagined.

Welcome to the right-hand side of the missing middle (see figure 6-1), where machines augment humans. Artificial intelligence tools are empowering workers in a range of fields, from design to medicine to engineering to factory-floor operations. This augmentation comes in a variety of forms—from augmented reality and virtual reality to analytics engines to robot arms and chatbots. But what are the workforce implications of being empowered or augmented by AI? How is introducing AI to a workplace

FIGURE 6-1

The missing middle—right side

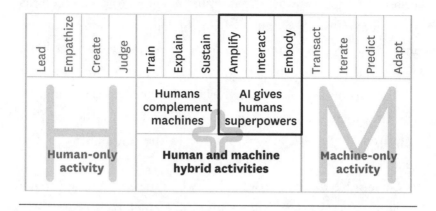

different from the device and technology management that companies already do, things like handing out laptops, software, and log-in information during new-hire orientation? This chapter argues that AI tools don't just automate routine workplace tasks— although they can do that, too—but that they create a symbiotic relationship between people and machines that upends the standard work flow. These new hybrid roles and relationships in the missing middle can offer managers an entirely new lens on their processes and equip people with powerful, new capabilities.

Three Types of Augmentation

AI augmentation and its reshaping of business processes is happening now, across the three categories of human-machine interaction: *amplification*, *interaction*, and *embodiment*.

In the case of *amplification*, AI agents give people extraordinary data-driven insights, often using real-time data. It's like your brain, but better.

The Elbo Chair example highlights some possibilities of *amplification*: generative design software expands the design space beyond what a person might be able to imagine. Other businesses are using worker-amplification tools for analyzing customers' sentiments when they interact with companies on Facebook and Twitter, for giving narrative writing advice, and for moderating online comments so internet conversations are constructive and civil. Drug companies are using amplification to monitor the quality control of pharmaceutical drugs after they've been released to the general population. And radiologists are getting help from software that learns the way they hang X-rays and provides patient health data in an easy-to-see format to speed up and improve the accuracy of diagnoses. These workers are all using AI to enhance the effectiveness of their activities and humans' decision-making process.

In the case of *interaction*, AI agents employ advanced interfaces such as voice-driven natural-language processing to facilitate interactions between people or on behalf of people. These AI agents are often designed to have a personality, and they can function at scale—that is, they can assist many people at once. You see them in personal assistant roles and in customer service. IPsoft's help-desk agent Amelia (called "Aida" in SEB's application, which is described in chapter 2) is an example of an AI agent that operates in the interaction domain.

Embodiment is the third category. While both amplification and interaction are mostly in the software realm, using interfaces that can, in some scenarios, seem almost invisible, embodiment is in tangible, physical spaces. It's AI in combination with sensors, motors, and actuators that allow robots to share workspace with humans and engage in physically collaborative work. These robots are on factory floors and in warehouses with people. They come in the form of robot appendages, package-carrying autonomous carts, and drones that deliver medicine.

Car companies, in particular, are using the concept of embodiment in their state-of-the-art manufacturing lines. Thanks to lightweight, context-aware robot arms and "cobots" designed to work closely with people on the line, manufacturers are able to reimagine previously static processes. Meanwhile, workers take on new roles when they collaborate with these smart machines, and businesses can make more varied, adaptable choices about the kinds of products they offer their customers.

In all three types of missing-middle interactions— amplification, interaction, and embodiment—companies are gaining not only super-powered employees but also a whole new way of thinking about the ways they run their businesses. AI augmentation allows workers to perform more human, less robotic activities. As certain tasks shift from human to machine, and humans, often working with AI assistants, are able to perform different kinds of work, companies are prompted to reimagine their business processes around entirely new human-machine capabilities. What's more, new augmentation-based relationships demand new kinds of human-computer interfaces. What user interfaces (UI) will dominate in the missing middle? Is AI the new UI? How might augmentation affect your industry? This chapter provides examples of companies that have reimagined their processes around machine-enabled superpowers and addresses some of these questions along the way.

AI Agents That Amplify

Autodesk's Dreamcatcher software uses genetic algorithms to iterate through possible designs. It offers a great example of the way a process changes when a smart agent is at a worker's side. Traditionally, when a designer wants to create a new object—a chair, a bike stem, an airplane partition—she starts by conducting research, sketching ideas, and moving between sketches, computer models, and physical prototypes. There are many iterations, during which the designer is making mental calculations, the equivalent of qualitative hunches, that nudge designs in one direction or another. (See figure 6-2.)

With AI, these mental calculations are offloaded to software, which enables the design process to be reimagined so that it can more fully focus on human creativity and aesthetics. Here, the designer begins by setting parameters, and the software proceeds to move through iterations at a quick pace. As the software produces its designs, the designer can further refine her parameters to see where it might lead the outcome. She's essentially steering the design, ultimately deciding on the final design. The process changes, then, from something that's somewhat clunky, slow, and limited (depending on other resources available to the designer), to one in which the designer is more often enacting her most valuable skill—her judgment and design sense. This adaptive and organic approach contrasts with the traditional design process, which was governed by iterations of predetermined steps.

Of course, it's not just designers whose work and processes are getting a boost from AI. Philips has a software tool for radiologists

FIGURE 6-2

Jobs with amplification

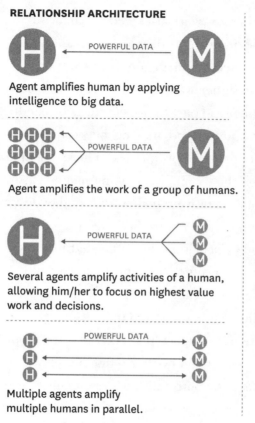

RELATIONSHIP ARCHITECTURE

POWERFUL DATA

Agent amplifies human by applying intelligence to big data.

POWERFUL DATA

Agent amplifies the work of a group of humans.

POWERFUL DATA

Several agents amplify activities of a human, allowing him/her to focus on highest value work and decisions.

POWERFUL DATA

Multiple agents amplify multiple humans in parallel.

EXAMPLE ACTIVITIES

Matching:
- Match resources, Q&A tasks
- Automate repetitive or low-level tasks

Recommending:
- Rank or design alternatives
- Prioritize resources
- Automate process change

Patterning:
- Identify trends in real time
- Personalize offerings
- Identify anomalies
- Categorize and route data
- Augment strategic decisions

called Illumeo. One of the software's features is that it includes contextual information about a patient alongside the images, so a radiologist doesn't have to hunt for laboratory results or prior radiology reports, for instance. But perhaps most impressively, the software is context aware in a number of areas. For instance, it can recognize the anatomy of the radiological images and automatically suggest the correct tool set—such as one that can measure and analyze blood vessels. The software is also able to learn how the radiologist prefers to look at the images, what's known as a radiologist's hanging protocol. Illumeo is a good example of how AI agents can slide into a preexisting interface—silently observing and learning the preferences of the person using a software tool, for instance, and incorporating that personalized information into the user experience. Illumeo is leveraging AI in its UI so that the relationship between worker and machine is adaptable and improves over time.[3]

So far, we've focused on amplification in office jobs, but workers in the field are also benefiting from amplification, thanks to AI-enhanced user interfaces. In particular, AI tools like smart glasses that provide an experience of augmented reality are overhauling maintenance work and in-field training: the glasses overlay digital information or instructions on a worker's field of view.

At a global industrial services company, the typical process for wiring a wind turbine's control box requires a technician to move between the control box and the hard copy of an instruction manual. But with an augmented-reality-enabled (AR), hands-free, heads-up display, the instructions can be visually projected on top of a technician's workspace. In a side-by-side comparison with the traditional instruction manual method, the AR headset was found to improve the worker's performance by 34 percent on first use. With no need to spend time ramping up or training to use the new technology, efficiency gains are immediate. A similar example from Boeing demonstrates efficiency improvements of 25 percent, and other cases show an average productivity improvement of 32 percent.[4]

Agents of Interaction

We first described Aida in chapter 2, where it was a part of the virtual help desk at the Swedish bank SEB. Over time, SEB trained and tested Aida to the point where the bank was confident enough in the system to allow it to be part of the processes that

AI at Airbus

Designers at Airbus used Dreamcatcher's AI capabilities to redesign a partition that separates the passenger compartment from the galley in the cabin of an A320. Engineers wanted the partition to be lightweight (to save fuel, so the plane would have a smaller carbon footprint), yet strong enough to anchor two jump seats for flight attendants. On the computer screen, designers watched the software cycle through thousands of bizarre, unexpected designs for the internal structure of the partition. The engineers ended up trusting one of the weird-looking ones. Instead of looking like a solid panel designed by professionals, the final partition looked more like a child's scribbles in a coloring book, while still meeting the criteria for strength, weight, and manufacturability.

Part of the reason the structure seemed so odd was that the genetic algorithm was seeded with a starting pattern that, similar to the Elbo Chair, was based on biological structures. It used slime molds because they efficiently connect to multiple points of contact, and mammalian bones that grow dense at contact points and light and airy elsewhere. Even though the resulting structure looked like a random hash of lines, it was optimized to be strong and light and minimize the material used. Then the engineers built it. Airbus's team 3-D printed more than a hundred separate partition pieces, made of high-strength metal alloy, and put it all together. After stress tests and a certification test with aviation authorities, the new partition could appear in planes by 2018.[a]

a. "Reimagining the Future of Air Travel," Autodesk, http://www.autodesk.com /customer-stories/airbus, accessed October 25, 2017.

interacts directly with its one million customers. Aida is now the first point for customers contacting SEB. The software can answer FAQ-type questions, guide users through a process, perform actions within internal systems, and ask follow-up questions to solve a user's problem. Crucially, when Aida encounters a question it can't confidently resolve, it connects to human experts and learns from their interaction with a customer.[5] (See figure 6-3.)

There are, of course, a variety of interaction agents available for use. As natural-language processing software evolves, it's becoming more and more feasible to plug in such agents to existing processes. Some examples are Microsoft's Cortana; Nuance Communications' Nina chatbot; and IBM's Watson, a

FIGURE 6-3

Jobs with interaction

RELATIONSHIP ARCHITECTURE

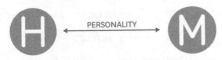

Human interacts with agent, administering work through a natural interface.

Agent interacts on behalf of many people, deferring to those people if necessary.

EXAMPLE ACTIVITIES

Administering:
• Automate Q&A
• Enable human workers to focus on high-value interactions

Coaching:
• Nudge for next best action based on domain expertise or corporate policy
• Accelerate understanding of customer and process context to solve problem

Conversing:
• Allow for voice-powered access to services and analytics
• Allow natural-language querying, commands, and sophisticated improvisation during dialogue

natural-language AI system that's used for various applications from banking and insurance to travel and health. At Accenture, for instance, Alice is an agent that uses Watson to answer common requests, and Colette is another Watson-based agent that answers home buyer's questions about mortgages.

Interaction agents needn't simply be a voice on the phone or an icon on a computer screen. Some agents have physical forms as well. By now, most people are familiar with consumer-facing, natural-language gadgets like Amazon's Alexa, Google Home, and Apple's Siri. But there are others; BQ Zowi, a squat, table-top robot originally designed for children, has open architecture and re-programmability that makes it ripe for various other uses. It's now able to answer questions for some banking customers via chatbots. Similarly, the small humanoid robot Nao uses IBM Watson's Q&A service to answer questions about banking, travel, and health, and technical queries about the company's systems, applications, and products.

In these examples of interaction, the software or robotic agent has access to vast stores of data and uses a natural-language interface to quickly access and disseminate that information. Companies that serve the needs of many customers at once can benefit from interaction modality in the missing middle. When interaction is well understood, it can revamp the customer service process, not only in customer service centers, but at points of sale and inside consumers' homes. Interaction can also alleviate previously tedious, repetitive tasks for workers. Once these tasks are gone, management and leadership can reimagine workers' processes around unusual, interesting, more nuanced customer service situations.

Rubbing Elbows with Robots

Amplification and interaction are missing-middle categories that mostly augment the mind. Embodiment, in contrast,
deals with physical augmentation. Examples are often found in
manufacturing, such as in the Mercedes-Benz plant in south-
west Germany. This facility processes fifteen hundred tons of
steel a day, pumping out more than four hundred thousand
vehicles a year. With these numbers, you might expect a well-
oiled, robot-dominated assembly line operating with as few
people as possible. But Mercedes is ditching some of its robots
and redesigning its processes to center them around people.
The automotive assembly line is changing. (See figure 6-4.)

The driver of this change is the rise of customizable cars.
You can now go online and choose from an expansive array of

FIGURE 6-4

Jobs with embodiment

RELATIONSHIP ARCHITECTURE

 PHYSICAL AID

Human collaborates with embodied robot
to augment physical work or navigation.

EXAMPLE ACTIVITIES

Navigating and extending:
- Self-navigate around humans
  and autonomous machines
- Extend sight, hearing,
  or touch

**Collaborating
in physical space:**
- Assist on very precise,
  arduous, or routine
  physical work

---

features on your next car. Gone are the days of identical Model Ts coming off an assembly line. Even the trend to make cars in three standard trims—common in the United States—is falling out of favor.

With so much variation in car manufacturing, the only way to assemble cars fast enough is to bring people back. "We're moving away from trying to maximize automation, with people taking a bigger part in industrial processes again," says Markus Schaefer, head of production planning at the Mercedes. "When we have people and machines cooperate, such as a person guiding a part-automatic robot, we're much more flexible and can produce many more products on one production line. The variety is too much to take on for the machines."[6]

Instead of dividing manufacturing plants into a heavy-lifting robot section, usually fenced off from people for safety reasons, and another area for people to dexterously fiddle with wires and perform more delicate tasks, a new breed of cobots is enabling humans and robots to work side by side or in collaboration. These cobots are built with smart software that learns over time and sensors that allow it to adapt to the situation at hand and be responsive to people. In practice, this means that the cobot takes on repetitive and precision tasks as well as the heavy lifting, while a person brings the brains and dexterity to the operation. Cobots, in this way, are literally extending the workers' physical capabilities.

Research from MIT corroborates that this kind of human-machine collaboration is effective for business. In a study with Mercedes' competitor BMW, researchers determined that human-robot interactions in the car plant were about 85 percent more productive than either humans or robots on their own.[7]

At the Mercedes plant, a worker grabs a console with buttons and a visual display, which he uses to guide a robot arm to pick up a heavy wedge of steel that will make up the floor of a car's trunk. The robotic system is equipped with sensors to see its environment and software that can quickly deliver instructions to the robot's actuators if, for instance, a person steps in the way or the car isn't perfectly positioned. This type of cobot system has the worker in control, guiding the building of each car. Industrial work becomes decidedly less manual and more like being a pilot, where the robot becomes an extension of the worker's body.[8]

The cobot arrangement is good for manufacturing because it allows for flexibility and adaptability in processes, and it appears to be good for people, too. One worker who collaborates with cobots at SEW-Eurodrive, a manufacturer of motors, describes the work environment: "This is more satisfying because I am making the whole system. I only did one part of the process on the old line."[9]

Cobots are good for human ergonomics, too. At a BMW plant in South Carolina, engineers analyzed their car-making processes to see how a lightweight robot arm could fit alongside its peopled production line. They found that the act of fixing the door panel, which safeguards the electrical wiring, is best done by a cobot on the line. Previously performed by humans, it was a task that had produced wrist strain. What's more, people seemed to be less consistent at the task than they were at others.[10]

Now a person loosely fits the door panel and then the door moves along the line to the nearby cobot to finish the job. The cobot is outfitted with cameras and other sensors so it can tell when a person is close. Unlike traditional industrial robots that perform set movements over and over without awareness of their surroundings, the cobot in the BMW plant deftly avoids knocking into people or getting in the way. Furthermore, these robots can be reprogrammed by nonprogrammers using a tablet. No coding skills are needed. And because they are lightweight, they can be moved anywhere in a warehouse and perform various tasks, depending on the need.[11]

The human-robot system then acts as an extender of people's ability to work; they're now less likely to get fatigued or injured. Suddenly a factory job isn't only for workers in their physical prime. Embodiment, as demonstrated in the human-robot systems that many manufacturers are using, is opening up more job opportunities: some people who may have ruled out manual labor as a work option—because of age or physical condition—may be able to do the work with the aid of cobots.

A similar collaborative dynamic is on display at warehouses. At Amazon fulfillment centers, shelves full of merchandise seem to independently glide down the warehouse aisles toward a human worker who's awaiting the delivery. The shelves are carried by squat, rolling robots destined to bring the goods to the worker, who plucks the items off the shelves and puts them in a box to ship. Computer vision helps the robots know where they are in the warehouse, sensors keep them from running into each other, and machine-learning algorithms help them determine the best paths and right-of-ways on a warehouse floor full of other robots. The human worker no longer needs to walk miles a day to retrieve goods for packaging.

In another example of embodiment, drones are being tested to deliver health care, on demand, to remote parts of Rwanda, out of reach of traditional medical options. A company called Zipline is pioneering the technology, targeting one of the leading causes of death—postpartum hemorrhage—with a delivery of blood for transfusion.[12]

Drones have become a particularly interesting application of AI: computer vision and smart algorithms process video in real time, thereby allowing people to extend their vision and delivery capabilities up into the air and over miles of potentially impassable terrain.

In a project similar to Zipline, Doctors Without Borders has experimented with using a small quadcopter drone from a company called Matternet. The drone takes lab samples of patients with suspected tuberculosis from remote health centers in Papua New Guinea to a major hospital for testing.[13] Another organization called Wings for Aid is using unmanned drones to drop off supplies in difficult-to-reach areas when a natural disaster has struck.[14]

In the near term, at least, it looks as if some of the most effective ways that robots can be deployed are in conjunction with people. Robots are skilled at heavy lifting and are superb at repetitive tasks. People are good at adapting on the fly, making judgment calls, and using their hands to manipulate wires, textiles, or other tricky materials. The collaboration between the two is changing the way industries think about their people and their processes.

From Task Replacement to Process Change

In all three categories on the right side of the missing middle—amplification, interaction, and embodiment—we see that AI offers significant improvements to the way people work, giving them new superpowers. Combine this with the three categories on the left side of the missing middle—training, explaining, and sustaining, which highlight the ways that workers improve the effectiveness of AI—and we start to see the coming shift.

To tap the full potential of a human-machine workplace, organizations need to recognize that these six new ways of working demand a complete reimagination of business processes. Specifically, when a designer can choose from thousands of unexpected and unusual chair designs—all retaining important structural requirements—AI has opened up a universe of creative options that was previously closed. When a carmaker can reimagine its factory floor so that people and robots are working in concert, AI has not only facilitated the creation of highly customized cars at scale, requiring a designer that must have the training and skills to take advantage of that freedom—it has essentially transformed the assembly line into a collaborative robot-human workspace.

In some situations, as with the technicians who wear heads-up displays while wiring wind-turbine boxes, these innovations can reduce the time it takes to get the job done by a third. But in others, as with Stitch Fix, mentioned in the introduction to part two, entirely new business models are emerging on the backs of AI technologies. When AI augments workers, we don't just see small, incremental revenue bumps or efficiency gains. We see safer, more engaged workers who can do the work well that they do best. In organizations, AI augmentation opens up the possibility to fundamentally rethink business processes to uncover hidden gains, embolden workers, and discover brand-new business models for this new age. But what are the managerial implications for companies deploying such innovations? How do you train and educate people for the new kinds of workplace interactions? What new skills are needed to work well with AI? The next two chapters look at these and other questions through the lens of MELDS. Chapter 7 will focus on mindset, experimentation, leadership, and data; chapter 8 will concentrate on skills.

7

A Leader's Guide to Reimagining Process

Five Steps to Getting Started

n the previous two chapters, we've taken a deep dive into the
missing middle—how on one side of the middle, humans
are building and managing machines, and on the other side
of the middle, machines are effectively giving humans superpowers. The missing middle concept undergirds our thinking
about how humans and machines work best together in the age
of AI; it's critical to reimagining business processes. But the
big question remains: *What are the actual steps for reimagining
business processes?* How should managers proceed?

Based on our observations of companies at the forefront of
implementing advanced AI technologies, we have uncovered five
key management practices. While we are still in the early days
of AI-driven business transformation, we believe these practices
provide a path forward. The five practices are each components

of the MELDS framework described in the introduction. We'll focus on the first four here:

- Executives must adopt the proper *mindset*, with a focus on not just improving business processes but rather on completely reimagining business processes and the way that work is performed.

- They need to foster a culture of AI *experimentation* that allows them to quickly realize how and where the technology can change a process, and where it makes sense to increase the scale and scope of a process.

- They must exercise the proper *leadership* in promoting responsible AI by managing the trust, legal, and ethical concerns that accompany AI and by considering the societal consequences of some process changes.

- Executives need to recognize the crucial importance of *data*, not just their firm's own AI-enabling data but also the broader landscape of available data.

In short, this chapter focuses on the "MELD" part of our MELDS framework (and in the following chapter we'll concentrate on the *skills*, or "S," part). We will provide examples of how leading companies are now implementing the above four practices and, along the way, we'll offer guidance to management and leadership aiming to implement AI in a way that fosters long-term growth. Our framework goes beyond what is typically found in IT and business-transformation methodologies, specifically addressing advanced AI and its accompanying issues, including those that tend to be neglected such as corporate culture, ethics, consumer trust, and employee trust.

1. Mindset: Imagine Processes That Might Be

Reimagination requires a completely different mindset—"a rupture with the world we take for granted," to borrow a phrase from technology researcher Shoshana Zuboff.[1] It is exactly such "ruptures" with the way things are currently done that enable companies to imagine novel business models and develop game-changing innovations. That is, when people simply accept an existing process and then use AI to automate it, they can achieve incremental improvements but little more. To attain step-level performance gains, they need to envision those ruptures—novel ways that work might be accomplished—and then figure out how to deploy AI to make those ruptures a reality. To accomplish this objective, we recommend that executives use this three-step method: discover and describe, co-create, and scale and sustain.

Discover and Describe

When trying to reimagine a process, it's natural for people to become stuck on the old way of doing things, making it difficult for them to envision things that might be. To avoid that, they should always keep in mind the difference between traditional business processes versus the new, AI approach. Our research shows that outcomes are no longer linear but exponential. Change is no longer episodic and human-led; it's self-adaptive, based on real-time input from humans as well as machines. Roles are not just limited to human-only and machine-only positions; they must also include collaborative work in the missing middle. And decisions don't only occur where work is performed by people; they must also take place where humans and machines collaborate.

With that new perspective, executives can begin discovering and describing what a reimagined process would be like. One effective means is to deploy a methodology like design thinking or empathic design to identify a product or process user's true needs. The goal is to transform the customer experience into providing a novel product or service to meet those needs. Of particular importance are any "pain points" in the customer experience. By first identifying those problem areas, managers can then think about ways to resolve them through the use of AI and real-time data. Many of these pain points might not have been practical or even possible to address in the past—the cost of a solution may have been prohibitive or the technical capabilities nonexistent. But today, given the advanced state of AI technologies, companies might now be able to resolve those very same pain points that had plagued them in the past.

Opportunities for reimagining processes can arise both inside as well as outside the organization. The pain point might be a cumbersome, lengthy internal process (for example, an HR department taking an inordinate amount of time to fill staff positions), or it might be a frustrating, time-consuming external process (for example, customers having to file multiple forms to get a medical procedure approved by their insurer). Often, identifying such opportunities for process reimagination is an iterative process.

Consider the case of a large agricultural company that was developing an AI system to help farmers improve their operations. The system would have access to an enormous amount of data from a variety of sources, including information on soil properties, historic weather data, etc. The initial plan was to build an application that would help farmers better predict their crop yields for upcoming seasons. However, through further research and observation the company learned of a more pressing issue that AI systems could address: Farmers really wanted real-time, adaptive recommendations. They wanted actionable, specific advice such as which crops to grow, where to grow them, how much nitrogen to place in the soil, and so on. Having discovered the farmers' real pain point, the company then developed a system and tested it on about a thousand fields. The initial outcomes were promising as farmers were happy with the crop yields they had obtained. Data from that initial test was then used to improve the algorithms.

The lesson here is that identifying opportunities for reimagination takes time—executives must capture the current business context, distill insights from various observations, and identify the potential value impact of the reimagined process. One person who worked on that crop-recommendation system had this advice: "You need to be extremely curious and patient until you're sure that you have absorbed sufficient domain knowledge, as well as a sufficient understanding of the available data."

It should be noted that AI itself can be very useful in augmenting an one's own powers of observation to spot previously hidden patterns of opportunity in the data. A manager could, for example, use advanced machine-learning algorithms to sift through hundreds of data sources, including customer emails, social media posts, and digital exhaust to identify where process reimagination could be most effective in removing a major customer pain point. (In chapter 3, we discussed the use of AI in sharpening a firm's powers of observation.)

Co-create

Identifying opportunities for process reimagination is one thing; pursuing them requires something else: the ability to envision work in the missing middle. To develop new mental models of how work might be done, executives should encourage co-creation among the stakeholders involved.

Put yourself, for example, in the place of a technician at an Audi dealership, and you come across an engine problem you can't solve. Your next step would be to call Audi of America's technical help line. This help line fields about 8,000 calls per month from more than 290 dealers across the country. Most of the time, remote technicians can troubleshoot problems over the phone. But in about 6 percent of cases, an expert technician needs to go to the dealership in person, says Jamie Dennis, Audi director of product quality and technical service. The solution is effective but not exactly efficient. Travel time can take between two hours to two days. All the while, the customer waits.[2]

The problem is that the need for expert technicians isn't going away anytime soon. Even though cars are becoming more reliable, they are also becoming more digitally complex, meaning that mechanics now have to be IT specialists, too. The combination of increased reliability and increased complexity means that most dealer technicians don't have many opportunities to solve some of the more challenging technical problems that arise in newer models. While this might help explain why customers could on occasion have to wait hours (or days) to get their cars fixed, it does little to ease their frustrations. So, what's the best way to train mechanics, and is there a better way to deploy expert technicians to remote dealerships to minimize customer wait times?

Audi found the answer through co-creation in the missing middle. The company deployed a fleet of telepresence robots called Audi Robotic Telepresence (ART) that not only helps train technicians in diagnostics and repair, but also speeds up the time it takes to make repairs in the first place. It's an example of employee amplification along with AI-enabled training, combined into a whole new process. With ART, the expert technician doesn't need to travel; instead, his or her voice and face are beamed across miles and emitted from ART's speakers and high-resolution display. The expert technician, in his office, remotely controls a robot that rolls, swivels, sees, hears, and scoots right up next to a technician on-site as he or she peers under the hood. The mobile robot has various vision sensors to ensure safe operation, which then helps establish a sense of trust with the humans it works alongside. Moreover, the video and voice communication network between the expert and technician is supported by AI behind the scenes to enhance collaboration between the mechanic and the remote, robotically embodied technician. It's almost as good as having someone watch over your shoulder as you lower a borescope into an engine cylinder to check on wear and tear. The expert technician can, in real time, offer advice on improving diagnostic and repair techniques. Dealer technicians learn on the fly; expert knowledge can be deployed instantly, across the country; and customers get their cars fixed faster. This innovative solution was made possible through co-creation, involving the expert technicians, mechanics, and AI technologists. Throughout the pilot project, for instance, standard protocols needed to be modified, and technicians helped by providing continual feedback for what was working and what wasn't.

Scale and Sustain

The final step of the reimagination process requires executives to scale their solution and sustain it with continual improvements. Audi, for example, commenced in June 2014 with an experimental pilot program for ART, which was carried out in 68 dealerships. Thanks to the success of that effort, by 2016 the company had plans to roll out the robots in all its US dealerships by the end of that year.[3] Another approach is to test a new system internally on employees to work out all the kinks before implementing the application externally to customers. That was the strategy of the Swedish bank SEB when it developed its virtual assistant, Aida, which as we discussed in chapter 2, was first deployed as a help-desk agent to assist 15,000 SEB employees before being rolled out to the bank's one million customers. And it's also the strategy used with Amazon Go, which we'll discuss in the next section.

2. Experimentation: Imagine an Experiment

In Seattle, there's a convenience store where you can walk in, grab a green juice, and walk out. No cashier rings you up. You don't even have to bumble your way through a self-checkout kiosk. Instead, cameras monitor you and your fellow shoppers as well as the items removed from shelves. Your juice bottle carries an embedded sensor that talks to your phone, charging your account. And just like that, the process of buying groceries has become automated. The store is called Amazon Go, and by the spring of 2017, it was serving a limited number of people—Amazon employees, mostly—as a way to prove the concept that it's possible to make shopping in physical stores almost as easy as clicking the Buy Now option on the Amazon website.[4]

Amazon Go is clearly an example of a bold retail experiment, and it also highlights something else: Amazon fosters a culture of experimentation. It allows crazy ideas to flourish. It designs, funds, and runs tests. Many of those will fail, but that's not the point. "I've made billions of dollars of failures at Amazon.com. Literally," Jeff Bezos says. "What matters is companies that don't continue to experiment or embrace failure eventually get in the position where the only thing they can do is make a Hail Mary bet at the end of their corporate existence. I don't believe in bet-the-company bets."[5] Instead, Bezos firmly believes in the incredible power of experimentation. (For another example of experimentation in a retail setting, see the sidebar "Controlled Chaos.")

Build-Measure-Learn

The technologies that power Amazon Go—computer vision, sensor fusion, and deep learning—are systems very much under development. Limitations include cameras that have a hard time tracking loose fruits and vegetables in a customer's hands and difficulty recognizing a customer who pulls his hat low or puts on a scarf that obscures her face. These behaviors, inadvertently or on purpose, spoofed the system during the Amazon Go test run in Seattle. But the only way to push the state of the

Controlled Chaos

Walmart's Store No. 8 is an "incubator," a place to house engineers and innovators who test new technologies—such as robotics, virtual and augmented reality, machine learning, and kinds of artificial intelligence—relevant to Walmart's business. Announced in March 2017, Store No. 8 will operate in many ways like any other startup incubator, experimenting with ideas and helping businesses "pivot" as concepts are tried and fail. According to Marc Lore, founder of Jet.com, a company Walmart bought in 2016 for $3 billion, the businesses and innovations forged in Store No. 8 "will be ring-fenced by the rest of the organization and backed by the largest retailer in the world."[a] In other words, it will have the financial resources of a giant corporation, and the freedom, isolated from the bureaucracy of a large corporate culture, of a startup. Store No. 8 plans to facilitate collaborations with outside startups, venture capitalists, and academics to develop a line of proprietary robotics,

a. Laura Heller, "Walmart Launches Tech Incubator Dubbed Store No. 8," *Forbes*, March 20, 2107, https://www.forbes.com/sites/lauraheller/2017/03/20/walmart-launches-tech-incubator-store-no-8/.

technology forward is to explore its edges. So, as a stop-gap to ensure quality control, Amazon employs people to watch video and scan images to make sure the cameras are tracking items and charging customers appropriately (sounds like trainers and sustainers, doesn't it?). The store is an example virtual and augmented reality, machine learning, and artificial intelligence technology. It has a wide-open mandate to do so.[b]

Named after the Arkansas center where Walmart founder Sam Walton was known to fiddle with new ideas, Store No. 8 is a reminder that Walton had a reverence for collecting data about his stores and experimenting with new ideas. But as companies grow in size, and especially if they were founded before digital technologies revolutionized most retail, they are often awkwardly positioned to move quickly and embrace new technologies such as AI. With the development of the in-house incubator, Walmart seems to acknowledge the difficulty and importance of injecting experimentation into its organization. Indeed, the acquisition of Jet.com, an online retailer, was mostly a bid to cross-stitch digital culture into the preexisting corporate fabric. And in the process, Store No. 8 is creating an environment where testing is encouraged and the wagers are large, but nobody's betting the farm.

b. Phil Wahba, "Walmart Is Launching a Tech Incubator in Silicon Valley," *Fortune*, March 20, 2017, http://fortune.com/2017/03/20/walmart-incubator -tech-silicon-valley/.

of human-in-the-loop automated processes, with the goal of improving a system to perform more accurately and autonomously before deploying to a broad customer base.

The company decided to not only test the concept in-house, but launch a store that had high-volume traffic. Critically, it selected its own employees as the test market. Its employees, already steeped in the company's use of minimal viable products and A/B testing techniques to understand customer needs, provide helpful feedback and, unlike regular customers, aren't put off if the technology occasionally fails. Companies that deployed IPsoft's Amelia, the AI assistant, used similar approaches: employees used the technology internally as the kinks were smoothed out; only later was it deployed for customers after a certain level of quality control was achieved.

Amazon shows that it's savvy about how managers apply its most cutting-edge AI and how its trainers and sustainers help implement and test it. Because he's fostered a culture of experimentation, Bezos has a secret weapon in innovation: a huge number of employees who are comfortable working in the missing middle and managers who know how to handle the uncertainty that comes with new terrain.

Amazon has also used its soft rollout to understand the boundaries of customers' expectations in the trade-off between creepiness, privacy, and ease of use. When it first announced the store, many tech publications noted that there was a certain creepiness in having your identity and every move monitored and recorded when you walk into a store. But if other Amazon products, like the Echo, are any indication, customers soon get used to being monitored, especially in a limited context where they feel they have some control over the situation. With the Echo, for instance, people know their conversations aren't recorded unless they use the wake-up words "Alexa," "Amazon," "Echo," or "Computer." Moreover, the Alexa app provides a log of their recorded conversations, which customers can delete.

Swift adoption of the Echo demonstrates the speed with which people shift to new norms around the technology, especially if they feel they're getting a good value and they have a sense of some control. Similar user controls and transparent interfaces might eventually play a part in Amazon Go as well.

At the Amazon Go stores, planned to be ten thousand to forty thousand square feet, customers can choose to shop online and come to the store for pickup, or shop in a store for a traditional grocery experience. Grocery stores can be a complicated business, and to consider automating parts of the in-store experience requires a good understanding of which tasks are best for human workers, which tasks are best for machines, and which tasks are ripe for collaborative efforts. Amazon is currently trying to figure out just that right mix of human and machine capabilities. The company has reported that the number of employees at the Amazon Go stores will remain the same as at a regular convenience store even though cashiers will no longer be needed, so it remains to be seen what new human roles will be created.[6]

The age of standard business processes is over; companies can no longer aim to replicate the best-in-class process of an industry leader. That's why experimentation is key. To compete, managers must tailor processes to the idiosyncrasies of their own businesses. The catch, though, is that tailor-made processes require managers and leaders to be more aware of their workforce and culture at large so they know how and when to implement experiments. For instance, to get buy-in from employees, leaders need to provide clear objectives and not discourage mistakes or missteps. After all, in science, an experiment that doesn't support the hypothesis isn't called a failure. It's called data.

3. Leadership: Imagine a Blended Culture of People and Machines

A big leadership challenge for many companies is that they must establish an organizational culture that promotes responsible AI. This can be difficult to achieve because many people have an inherent distrust of technology, and those fears can often be exacerbated by workplace anxieties about job displacement. To help employees become more comfortable with their AI coworkers, managers need to use the roles and interactions found on both sides of the missing middle. The skills of trainers, explainers, and sustainers are absolutely crucial, as we'll see later. But just as important is fostering positive experiences with AI augmentation. Make it clear to employees that you are using AI to replace tasks and reimagine processes. Demonstrate that AI tools can augment employees and make their day-to-day work less tedious and more engaging.

Meanwhile, though, here's what businesses are facing. When discussing the safety of autonomous vehicles, Gill Pratt, chief executive of the Toyota Research Institute, told lawmakers on Capitol Hill in 2017 that people are more inclined to forgive mistakes that humans make than those by machines.[7] Research confirms the inconsistency and ambiguity with which we trust machines. A 2009 paper reported that when people thought their stock reports were coming from a human expert, their price estimates were more likely to be swayed than if they thought the information came from a statistical forecasting tool. Another paper from 2012 found that people assumed doctors' medical decisions were more accurate and ethical then those made by a computer. Even seeing evidence to the contrary tends not to sway opinions. A 2014 study found that "people more quickly lose confidence in algorithmic than human forecasters after seeing them make the same mistake." That same year, three researchers at the University of Pennsylvania coined the term that describes people's desire to put trust in other humans rather than machines: "algorithm aversion."[8]

The financial trading industry might be one of the most advanced business cultures in terms of interacting with algorithms. Yet, even here, algorithm aversion remains a key stumbling block. Systematica's Leda Braga launched the investment management firm in 2015; it focuses solely on algorithmic trading. While Braga concedes that roles remain for humans in trading—for instance, activists and short sellers whose work is based on deep research into fundamentals and management teams of companies—those roles are disappearing. She believes the future of finance is in automation. In the meantime, Systematica's approach encounters resistance, she says, which includes human preferences for human decision makers. "The stumbling block is the algorithm aversion," says Braga. For many applications, Braga contends, "We all prefer the human to do the job for us, even when the human does a worse job . . . [W]e have to get more rational."[9]

Clearly, some aversion is a good thing. Our own research, as well as a recent Pew Center study, suggests that managers should encourage a thoughtful balance of skepticism and acceptance amid the complex changes wrought by AI.[10] It helps to highlight some of the positives, such as the way banks might have more complete data to help grant loans with less bias, whereas in the past a banker's bias might have kept people from qualifying due to their race, gender, or postal code. Health-care providers, too, are seeing how AI can reduce costs when they use AI to offload or scale certain tasks that doctors couldn't manage for as many patients as they might have wanted.

Of course, we're still figuring out exactly what AI can and can't do, and how to best fit it into business processes. It's therefore unhelpful to blindly trust all AI equally. Sound human judgment remains a crucial part of implementing AI.

But from software bots to multi-jointed robot arms, AI has infiltrated businesses in a way that is changing job descriptions and redefining organization charts. So how can you foster a culture of trust that extends even to robo-colleagues? One way is to test with AI and train for it, as we discussed in the earlier "Experimentation" section of this chapter. Then, when a solution is ready for prime time, you can also deploy some of the following basic tools and techniques to help foster trust and a bit more rationality.

Install Guardrails

One approach is to build guardrails into an AI-based process. These give managers or leadership control over outcomes that might be unintended. One example is Microsoft's chatbot named Tay. In 2016, Tay was introduced on Twitter as a bot that would learn from interactions with other Twitter users. Within hours, it had been trained to tweet vulgar, racist, and sexist language, and its creators had quickly removed it from the web.[11] What protections could Microsoft have used? Keyword or content filters or a program that monitored for sentiment could have provided a protective cushion. Similarly, in industry, it's good to know the boundaries of what your AI is and isn't allowed to do. Make sure others know the boundaries as well. In an organization, usually the sustainer asks about the boundaries, limitations, and unintended consequences of AI and then develops the guardrails to keep the system on track. Guardrails, therefore bolster worker confidence in AI.

Use Human Checkpoints

Ninety-two percent of automation technologists don't fully trust robots. Part of the problem is human uncertainty around what the robot is "thinking" or planning to do next—that the machine is an inscrutable black box. These same technologists (76 percent) suggest that the top solution is to use some sort of visual output that provides analytics and a dashboard with other metrics.[12] It's a simple solution that can reduce opacity in the system—and keep humans firmly in the loop. Here, the role of the explainer is key. Even if the entire mind of an AI system can't be known, some insights into its inner workings can be very beneficial. Explainers should understand both what's useful for people to see in a visualization and what's important for the system to share.

Minimize "Moral Crumple Zones"

For services like Uber, Lyft, and Amazon's Mechanical Turk, AI-based software is augmenting some management roles: it doles out tasks, gives feedback and ratings, and helps people track progress toward goals. AI-enhanced management is a necessary innovation if these companies' business models are to scale and employ hundreds of thousands of people world-wide. But while management can offload certain activities, it can't offload underlying responsibility for how they are administered.

This issue is complex, requiring managers to be deliberate and thoughtful in their design choices. As AI-enhanced managers reconfigure the relationship between company leadership, employees, and society, companies need to be aware of the bigger, more impactful, and potentially unintended consequences that come with these changes. We need new mechanisms to make sure people don't take the hit when AI-enhanced managers fail. To develop such mechanisms, though, we first need to understand the concept of the "moral crumple zone."

In a car, the crumple zone is the part of the vehicle that's designed to take a hit so the driver is less likely to be seriously injured. With certain kinds of AI management systems, it's the people—employees and customers—who take a hit when the system fails. This erodes trust.

Ethnographers Madeleine Clare Elish and Tim Hwange coined the phrase "moral crumple zone." In their research, they saw that, in our digital world, control of certain services like ride sharing has become distributed across multiple human and nonhuman actors, yet social and legal conceptions of responsibility remain the individual's alone.

In a 2016 report, Elish provides an example of the moral crumple zone in action.[13] She had summoned a ride-sharing service to take her to the airport in Miami. The driver selected the first option provided by the map app for the Miami airport, and off they went. Elish fell asleep and awoke to find that her driver, who was new to the platform, had taken her to a location twenty minutes away from the airport's passenger terminal. To get Elish to the airport on time for her flight, the driver needed to cancel the upcoming ride that the app offered and essentially provide Elish with a free ride, though he had no obligation to do so. He did it anyway, and Elish made her flight.

In this scenario, the service failed both the driver and the customer, but there was no straightforward way to register the negative experience. The main feedback options were for the driver and passenger to rate each other. But whose fault was it that the app supplied an incorrect address, the driver didn't know where he was going, and Elish fell asleep and didn't course-correct mid-ride?

Elish explains the moral crumple zone:

[T]he human in a highly complex and automated system may become simply a component—accidentally or intentionally—that bears the brunt of the moral and legal responsibilities when the overall system malfunctions. The metaphor of the moral crumple zone isn't just about scapegoating. The term is meant to call attention to the ways in which automated and autonomous systems deflect responsibility in unique, systematic ways. While the crumple zone in a car is meant to protect the human driver, the moral crumple zone protects the integrity of the technological system, itself.[14]

For algorithmically-managed crowd platforms, human operators can also become "liability sponges," getting bad feedback from a customer when it's really the system's fault, for instance. Additionally, they bear the brunt of expenses on their cars—the insurance, the gas, the wear and tear, all the while absorbing the liability on behalf of the ride-hailing app if something goes wrong with their ride-giving vehicle.

Here are some ways to address the current shortcomings. First, create ways for algorithms to be accountable and identify root causes so that they can be fixed. Accountability isn't just for human workers. Second, give human workers in the system the ability to second-guess the AI. Trust that workers have judgments and provide valuable context, and that they can provide quality assurance for the service. Third, allow rating systems to be used for algorithms or machines, not just for humans. Fourth, continually find where misalignments between control and responsibility are emerging. To fully address the problems that arise from developing systems that lead to moral crumple zones and liability sponges, companies need to spend significant effort realigning cultural values and norms.

Consider Legal, Psychological, and Other Issues

Start an ongoing conversation with your compliance department. AI can help with compliance—pulling reports, organizing data—but AI can also pose challenges. Sometimes adaptable AI systems produce unanticipated responses. Know how AI fits into existing risk management protocols and where to bolster the protocols to accommodate a dynamic AI decision maker. The roles on the left side of the missing middle—trainer, explainer, and sustainer—are valuable in this process.

More generally, when you give employees the ability to modify the outcome of an AI system—which allows them to feel like actors in a process, not simply cogs—they tend to more easily trust AI. Consider an engineer who's looking for a modest, attainable, 2 percent increase in the output of an oil well. She might turn to AI software to get the increase, adjusting software parameters, and closely monitoring the outcome. She might play the part of a sustainer, for instance, to make sure the software is working as intended. So, when she achieves her goal with the help of AI, she's also learning to trust the system. As research shows, giving users some control over the algorithm makes them more likely to feel the algorithm is superior and more likely to continue to use the AI system in the future.[15]

It's not always possible, though, to control the actual algorithms. Take the complicated task of assigning hospital beds to patients. One company developed a digital model of hospital beds and a patient-allocation scheme. An efficient hospital has 70 or 80 percent of its beds in use at any one time, but with the software, a hospital can assign 90 percent or more. Managers deployed the software in one hospital, expecting the theoretical 10 to 15 percent gain, but instead saw zero improvement. Upon investigation, they discovered that people dynamics were at play. For instance, a nurse who had been working with the same doctors in the ward for a long time was relying on experience to make decisions. So, when a recommendation for patient placement came up, the nurse just ignored it, not trusting the algorithm to do better.[16]

How did managers help the nurses learn to trust AI? By simply explaining why putting a certain patient in a certain bed was a good choice. (An explainer could participate in the design of the software interface, for instance, to include a brief explanation or rationale for bed assignments.) Managers discovered that, without being given an explanation, people are more likely to trust human judgment than an algorithm's recommendation. At the same time, managers found that they had to give those who assigned beds some leeway in the process, allowing them to have decision-making power as well.[17]

Overall, then, to engender trust in AI systems, leaders need to allow those who work with systems to develop stakes in the outcome and to have a sense of agency over the inner workings of the system, as in the example of the petroleum engineer. Ideally, AI systems should generally be designed to offer explanations of their decisions and to help people maintain some decision-making autonomy, as in the hospital-bed example. Developing processes that are fundamentally trust-based takes time and experimentation, but case studies show that if all parties are trusted—humans, machines, and humans and machines working together—then outcomes can improve for everyone.

4. Data: Imagine a Data Supply Chain

Good data is, first and foremost, fundamental to AI. In essence, it is the essential fuel that powers AI. To provide that necessary fuel, imagine data as an end-to-end supply chain. By this we mean a fundamentally new way of thinking about data, not as a static process that's managed separately in silos across the organization but as a dynamic enterprise-wide activity for capturing, cleaning, integrating, curating, and storing information. Because the data will be consumed by machine-learning, deep-learning, and other AI applications, it must be both rich (in terms of variety, quality, and usefulness) as well as big (in terms of sheer volume). It's important to remember here that AI systems are trained in feedback loops, such that the algorithms improve in tandem with both the quality and quantity of data. In other words, the systems will only be as good as the data that's been used to train them. As such, companies must focus on those missing-middle roles that help capture data and prepare it for analysis. These roles are crucial because biases in the data can have serious consequences, leading to skewed results and wrongheaded decisions. Today, about 90 percent of the time of people who train AI applications is spent on data preparation and feature engineering, rather than on writing algorithms.[18]

Although this is the fourth management practice, data awareness is what eventually enables action—and action is the operative word. Here are our action items.

Think Dynamically

Data supply chains must be dynamic, constantly evolving and continuously fueled by real-time data. Various new technologies, including those for data capture (sensors), storage, preparation, analysis, and visualization, can enable companies to acquire and consume data in novel ways.

Consider, for example, Ducati, the Italian designer and manufacturer of high-performance motorcycles. The company's racing team division—Ducati Corse—wanted to find a faster, cheaper, and more effective way of testing its race bikes, so it turned to AI. The intelligent testing system consists of an analytical engine that deploys machine learning and data-visualization tools that provide an intuitive user interface. Up to 100 IoT sensors on the bikes help provide a range of real-time data, including speed revolutions, brake temperatures, and so on.[19]

All that state-of-the-art technology enables the test engineers to interact easily with the system to probe insights and investigate how a bike will perform on different racetracks under various weather conditions. Now, the engineers can get more results from fewer on-track testing sessions, which saves time, effort, and money. And, thanks to the data and models, the system has been able to provide increasingly accurate performance predictions.

Obviously, building a dynamic data supply chain like Ducati Corse's takes considerable effort and resources, but you can kick off your process reimagination on a much smaller scale. Though data might be big and getting bigger, companies should focus on tackling well-defined, small-scale, early projects with their data. Choose a simple outcome to start, one in which AI can help you accomplish practical goals.

Tempo, the calendar application, has taken this approach. The iPhone app uses data from the phone itself such as social media, email, location, and more to "learn" about events. Then, it gives iPhone users just the event information at just the right time. Tempo manages a universe of complicated data, but the company kept its goal simple with event information only.[20] Don't be intimated by the scale of data you encounter. Focus on simple AI challenges first and move on from there.

Widen Access and Increase Variety

As your small AI experiments grow, work to ensure that your data supply chain is made up of disparate, readily accessible sources of data.

These days, managers might even have access to data they don't control or own. For example, if a regional grocery chain wants to analyze its daily transactions over the past month, it should look beyond the numbers in its database. Many companies already track sentiment on social media sites; they also analyze data in the context of weather, shoppers' characteristics, events in the news, or virtually any new data dimension imaginable—if they can locate the relevant data. Sometimes you can turn to data-as-a-service providers or open data sources (free to anyone to use in any way).

For example, Beiersdorf, a global provider of skin-care products, is using its own internal data along with syndicated data from research companies like Nielsen to provide board members with insights—in an act of amplification—about the development of various products and brands. The company plans to automate this process, leading to more accurate, faster insights.[21]

As companies work to increase the variety of their data sources, they should be aware of any barriers to the flow of that information. Some of these obstacles might be technical (for example, the organizational infrastructure might be insufficient for managing massive volumes of data), while others might be societal (specifically, the growing public distrust as firms accumulate and share increasing quantities of personal data).

Increase Velocity

Some data is fast: for example, a news event of a sudden natural disaster. This important and time-critical data needs to be accelerated throughout the supply chain. Slow data, on the other hand, is less relevant and could be much less useful. Historically, IT professionals have addressed the problem of mixed-speed data by giving preference to "hot" data, which is accessed frequently and saved on high-performance systems for quick retrieval. In contrast, "cold" data—tax records, for instance—can be stored on less zippy servers.

Facebook recognizes how to prioritize its data and revamp its processes accordingly. For instance, the social network discovered that 8 percent of all Facebook photos accounted for 82 percent of its network traffic. Photos, it seems, decrease in popularity the older they get. Facebook developed a three-tiered data storage solution. Its AI software labels photos and stores them in the appropriate tier. The more popular ones are stored on high-performance servers and can be pulled up instantly, while the less popular ones are stored on slightly slower, energy-saving servers. This way, customer satisfaction doesn't take a hit, and the company saves on energy costs.[22]

Enable Discovery

What kind of conversations are you having with your data? Are only analysts and data scientists benefiting from analysis tools? Your goal should be to extract insights in such a way that anyone, especially less-technical business users can take advantage of the story that the data is trying to tell.

Ayasdi is democratizing discovery, providing software that's useful to data scientists and non-technical business leaders alike. One of its customers, Texas Medical Center (TMC), focuses on the analysis of high-volume, high-dimensional data sets such as data from breast-cancer patients. Within minutes, the software is able to identify a new subset of survivors with certain common characteristics that may prove important.[23] TMC plans to use the company's tools for various applications, from analyzing clinical and genomic data to drug repurposing.[24] TMC's success shows that it pays to find analysis tools that democratize discovery so that you can enlist a diverse group of expert employees to help you develop your data experiments and reimagine your processes.

Fill the Missing Middle

A data supply chain requires more than just advanced technologies and a flow of good information. In addition, executives must design specific roles in the missing middle to develop and manage the system.

Note that AI feedback loops create dynamic, virtuous cycles of learning and improvement. As such, trainers are required to develop a curriculum for helping smart machines improve over time through those feedback loops of data and algorithms. Trainers at Google, for example, are working to improve a natural-language processing systems' ability to recognize local dialects. In that effort, trainers have already collected sixty-five thousand data points on thirty words (that is, different ways people pronounce those specific words).[25]

In addition to such trainers, explainers and sustainers are also needed as humans in the loop in order to guard against biases in the data supply chain. Many AI processes already have built-in mechanisms to help improve a system. When you take a different route than the one suggested by Waze, for example, that information helps refine that algorithm to make better recommendations in the future. Even so, biases can easily creep into a system. Software used to predict defendants' future criminal behavior, for example, has been shown to be biased against black defendants.[26] As such, companies that deploy advanced AI will always need explainers and sustainers to ensure the proper functioning of those systems. To address data biases and other related issues, Google has launched the PAIR (People + AI Research) initiative, and the company has released a set of open-source tools that can help organizations obtain a better view of the data used by their AI systems.[27]

Firms should also consider appointing a *data supply-chain officer*. This individual would be the top sustainer in the organization, overseeing all other sustainer roles. The data supply-chain officer would have the responsibility of constructing an integrated, end-to-end data supply chain, and would need to resolve the various issues involved. Where are the data silos? How can we simplify data access? What data is being underutilized, and how can we tap into any valuable "dark data"?

New Game

Obviously, reimagining a business process is no simple matter and, to be sure, many companies have stumbled in their attempts. Yet numerous firms have also succeeded, resulting in notable improvements in their businesses. What separates the two groups, we have found, is an adherence to four fundamental practices, each of which corresponds directly to the principles of our MELDS framework. The framework provides a comprehensive approach to implementing advanced AI systems, taking into account important issues like organizational culture, worker training, and employee trust that are often overlooked—or unexpected.

Specifically, to be successful at process reimagination, executives must first have the right *mindset* to envision novel ways of performing work in the missing middle, using AI and real-time data to observe and address major pain points. They should then focus on *experimentation* in order to test and refine that vision, all the while building, measuring, and learning. Throughout that process, though, they need to consider how to build trust in the algorithms deployed. That takes *leadership*—managers who promote responsible AI by fostering a culture of trust toward AI through the implementation of guardrails, the minimization of moral crumple zones, and other actions that address the legal, ethical, and moral issues that can arise when these types of systems are deployed. And last but certainly not least, process reimagination requires good *data*, and companies need to develop data supply chains that can provide a continuous supply of information from a wide variety of sources. All this, then, represents the MELD part of our MELDS framework.

In the next chapter, we explore the new set of fusion skills for people in the age of AI. By "fusion," we mean the combination of human and machine capabilities in the missing middle that enable firms to reimagine processes. This is the crucial *skills* part of MELDS, and we'll learn how changes in the skills necessary for success will have an impact on the future of work itself.

8

Extending Human + Machine Collaboration

Eight New Fusion Skills for an AI Workplace

Imagine you're a maintenance worker in a power plant, and you were just notified of unexpected wear and tear inside a turbine. If the notification system is run by GE's Predix software, which employs the digital-twin concept, you might even hear the alert spoken aloud as a computerized voice: "Operator, a change in my mission is causing damage to my turbine rotor."

You then ask for details, and the computer rattles off statistics that describe the way the turbine has been running over the past six months. The system also tells you that the damage has increased by four times, and if it continues, the rotor will lose 69 percent of its useful life. If you're wearing an augmented-reality headset, the computer will show you exactly where on the rotor the damage has occurred, marking the region with an angry red slash.

Ten years ago, you would have been lucky to catch this kind of damage on a routine maintenance check. A worst-case—but also likely—scenario is that no one would have detected the damage until the rotor broke and the turbine stopped spinning. But now, with sensors embedded throughout components and facilities, and with software that allows companies to digitally model it all and scan the status of operations, you can catch the problem before it requires a major repair or causes a costly shutdown.

With the damage identified, you ask the computer how to fix it, and the system provides maintenance options, including one that automatically and adaptively reduces stress on the rotor by modifying the way it's used. This recommendation is based on historical data, fleet data, and weather forecasts, among other factors, and the system has 95 percent confidence in its assumptions. But before you make a decision, you inquire about cost, and the computer tells you that the recommended course will generally save on fuel and electrical costs, and that you'll ultimately save an estimated $12 million by preventing an unplanned outage. Convinced after a ten-minute conversation with a computer, you instruct the system to proceed with the recommended option.[1]

What just happened? GE's AI-enabled software transformed a standard maintenance job into something wholly different from what it was just five years ago. It's the kind of AI deployment that's not just speeding up work tasks, but at its core, allows workers, managers, and executives to completely reimagine processes and what it means to work.

In our research, we see a strong recognition and embrace of the notion that work is changing in profound new ways. In our Accenture Research global survey on the Future of Work, done in collaboration with the World Economic Forum, we found that

64 percent of workers recognize that the pace of change is accelerating as a result of new technologies like AI. And while nearly all (92 percent) believe the next generation of workplace skills will look radically different, most (87 percent) believe new technologies like AI will improve their work experience within the next five years. Moreover, 85 percent of workers are willing to invest their free time over the next few years to learn new skills, while another 69 percent place a premium on finding on-the-job training opportunities where the training is relevant to the future digital needs of the enterprise.[2]

But what will be relevant in a world where the next generation of necessary skills bears little relevance to those of the past?

In our work and research, we see evidence of at least eight novel *fusion skills* (the "S" in our MELDS framework) that workers will need. Each skill draws on the fusion of human and machine talents within a business process to create better outcomes than working independently. What's different from previous eras of human-machine interaction, of course, is that the machines are learning from you as you learn from them, creating circles that continuously improve process performance.

In the case of the GE maintenance worker, you would need the ability to ask the machine smart questions across multiple levels of abstraction. We call this skill *intelligent interrogation*. As a maintenance worker using the GE's digital twin, you would start your interrogation with the troubled rotor but quickly scale up, asking questions about operations, process, and financial concerns. You aren't just a rotor expert; with the help of the digital twin, you've become an expert of a much more complex system; your knowledge of "how things work" has become ever more important.

We describe each of the eight fusion skills to guide managers and workers in designing and developing a workforce capable

FIGURE 8-1

Fusion skills for the missing middle

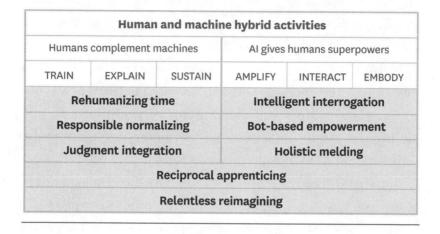

Human and machine hybrid activities					
Humans complement machines			AI gives humans superpowers		
TRAIN	EXPLAIN	SUSTAIN	AMPLIFY	INTERACT	EMBODY
Rehumanizing time			Intelligent interrogation		
Responsible normalizing			Bot-based empowerment		
Judgment integration			Holistic melding		
Reciprocal apprenticing					
Relentless reimagining					

of thriving in the missing middle (see figure 8-1). Three of these skills allow people to help machines (the left side of the missing middle); another three enable people to be augmented by machines (the right side of the missing middle); and the last two help people skillfully work across both sides of the missing middle. While these skills are about profound new forms of human-machine interaction, they don't require expertise in machine learning or programming or other technical areas. Rather, they require thoughtful humans who are eager to adapt these fundamental skills into the specific needs of their business.

FUSION SKILL #1: *Rehumanizing Time*

Definition: The ability to increase the time available for distinctly human tasks like interpersonal interactions, creativity, and decision making in a reimagined business process.

At the start of the industrial era, people had to get used to working on machine time. That is, they had to keep up with assembly lines and other automated processes. Then the idea of machine time was transferred to offices, as information technology and computers became integral to business processes in the 1990s. Industrialization and digital technologies radically changed the amount of time people spent working, writes Marina Gorbis of the Institute for the Future. A British peasant in the thirteenth century worked about 1,600 hours a year, for instance. A UK factory worker in the 1990s worked about 1,850 hours a year. And an investment banker in New York today works close to 3,000 hours. "By extending our capabilities, [machines] set new expectations for what's possible and create new performance standards and needs," Gorbis writes. "Before we created dishwashers, we didn't expect our glasses to be spotlessly clean, nor did we think dustless floors were necessary until we introduced vacuum cleaners into every home. Our tools change us."[3]

How is time changing again at the dawn of human-machine fusion? We've found that a new skill is emerging that allows for a new way of thinking about time and work. Rehumanizing time, in effect, allows people to skillfully redirect their time toward more human activities, such as increasing customer satisfaction, performing more complex machine repairs, or conducting creative, blue-sky research.

Medicine, in particular, is a field where rehumanizing time might have significant ramifications. Right now, physician burnout is on the rise. According to a 2015 study, 46 percent of doctors in 2011 reported at least one symptom of burnout, and by 2014, it jumped to 54 percent. There are serious consequences when doctors burn out or become depressed: they're more likely to make data-entry errors or other mistakes, which lead to poor outcomes.[4]

To squelch the burnout, the University of Pittsburgh Medical Center (UPMC) and Microsoft have partnered to see if AI can help. Tal Heppenstall, treasurer of UPMC, suspects that today's burnout issues track with the rise in digital medical records, which requires doctors to spend time performing data entry rather than seeing patients. "What they feel like and what they're burned out about is the fact that they're a slave to the computer, and it just shouldn't be that way," Heppenstall says.[5]

The UPMC-Microsoft partnership aims to use AI tools such as natural-language processing to listen in on doctor-patient conversations and transfer some of that information into forms and medical records. It would be like having a note-taking assistant standing by at every appointment, something few doctors have.

At Intel AI Day in 2016, experts from the Mayo Clinic, Penn Medicine, Kaiser Permanente, and Cigna came together to discuss the ways AI could change medicine. Overwhelmingly, the panelists agreed that AI is an ideal tool to reduce the load of rote tasks that doctors have. AI can help read X-rays and MRIs; it can find elevated risks of heart failure, buried in medical records when a routine exam might miss it; it can help identify cancerous moles that might go undetected. All these insights can give physicians back precious minutes of human-human interaction with their patients.[6]

It's clear that AI will significantly alter the intricately linked concept of work and time, but what's not clear is how the extra time that AI provides will be used. At AT&T, AI is finding lost hours in workers' days by pulling sales leads across multiple systems. This has freed up sales associates to spend more time developing relationships with customers instead of hunting through databases. But if managers and CEOs continue to operate in the paradigm of machine time, then workloads will likely increase. Doctors will continue to see more patients; customer service personnel will respond to more complaints and comments; mechanics might be fixing more robots than ever. There will likely be some productivity increases, but to truly reimagine processes means that businesses need to consider where the best returns on their workers' times might be. Would it make more sense to offer more employee training? What about allowing for volunteer or social-responsibility activities, which could benefit local communities and be good for a company's brand? What's known is that few people do their best work when they operate relentlessly at the edge of their productivity threshold. So as AI changes the nature of human-machine interaction, rehumanizing time reminds us that we have an opportunity to increase worker effectiveness and well-being, along with productivity.

FUSION SKILL #2: *Responsible Normalizing*

Definition: The act of responsibly shaping the purpose and perception of human-machine interaction as it relates to individuals, businesses, and society.

It's surprising how quickly you can get used to riding in an autonomous car. The first time you see its wheel turn on its own, you might shudder, but by the second right turn, it all starts to feel normal. Many people who have ridden in autonomous cars quickly conclude that driving is far too complex and dangerous a task for people to do. Unfortunately, autonomous cars are not yet widely distributed, and in many places, they're still misunderstood.

There's a gap between the use of AI technologies and the wide acceptance and understanding of them. Bridging this gap is where the skill of normalizing comes into play. Normalizing is about responsibly shaping the way people understand human-machine collaborations as well as the overall perception of them.

It's often most valuable when robots are introduced into public spaces like roads, hospitals, fast-food restaurants, schools, and nursing homes. Normalization requires a subset of other skills—understanding of humanities, STEM skills, an entrepreneurial spirit, public relations acumen, and an awareness of social and community issues.

Autonomous cars have been creeping up in our rearview mirrors for some time. In the early 2000s, DARPA organized a series of Grand Challenges to prompt researchers to develop robotic vehicles that could race against each other. DARPA's effort was one of the early steps in popularizing driverless cars. Fast forward to today, when Tesla offers Autopilot for its cars, and Audi has launched its A7 Sportsback, nicknamed Jack, which is programmed to drive with humanlike quirks such as slowing down or speeding up to let another car into its lane. Audi, in particular, has an ad campaign to normalize the concept of its "piloted driving" systems. The car company presents piloted driving as a human-machine collaboration, which recognizes that no car today is ready to fully drive itself all the time. At the same time, the car's technology is there to help. "In presenting our activities in the area of piloted driving, we had previously always placed the primary focus on technology and performance," says Michael Finke, head of the international creative department at Audi. "We are now addressing the subject from a completely different emotional side."[7]

CEOs will play a significant role in normalizing AI technologies to the public. Right now, the public is mostly neutral on AI, although many people operate with assumptions based on the human versus machine binary. Because of this, one major event—such as a child being killed by a driverless car, or truck drivers striking in opposition to the threat of self-driving trucks—can create a crisis of confidence in the technology at large. CEOs must anticipate resistance—through understanding the needs and concerns of communities affected by the changes wrought by AI—and find ways to ameliorate strife.

Normalization is equally important when introducing new AI to workers. One effect of normalization is that CEOs must develop a clear thesis on the future of work. Workers—a critical asset in any organization—can become allies in normalizing the technology if they feel executives and management address their concerns and if they have some say in the matter. A telecom executive told us that when AI came to the organization, the goal was clearly to use AI to make current workers more successful, not to lay them off. "Management is telling a good story about AI as a means of increasing revenue and saving costs as a means of growing the business and making it more competitive," he says. "So . . . a bigger pie means that people that are displaced by AI are re-skilled and move to other areas of the business as it grows."

FUSION SKILL #3: *Judgment Integration*

Definition: The judgment-based ability to decide a course of action when a machine is uncertain about what to do.

When a machine is uncertain about what to do, or lacks necessary business or ethical context in its reasoning model, people must be smart about sensing where, how, and when to step in. "With machine learning you are really disintermediating the human judgment, and the human's fault in the decision-making," says Adam Wenchel, Capital One's vice president of data innovation. "You are actually pulling them further and further out, and I think this is part of a shift that has been going on for a while."[8]

To bring human judgment back in the loop, Wenchel's team is applying and developing both statistical and soft skills. As machine-learning models evolve, learn, are retrained, and reused elsewhere in the business, they analyze "how they deviate from simple rule-based systems or from previous versions of the model." This analytics-based judgment informs employees where to set up guardrails, investigate anomalies, or avoid putting a model into customer settings.

On the intuition side, employees are encouraged to identify and voice concerns when something feels ethically problematic or off-track. Even when "your model is returning very good results and very good accuracy," people need to be comfortable and capable to jump in and say, "'Hey, we may be getting great accuracy . . . , but I have concerns of how we are getting there,'" Wenchel says.[9]

Despite all the remarkable advances in AI that we've seen throughout *Human + Machine*, artificial intelligence still has a framing problem.[10] AI can get many things right, but it still doesn't know how to read situations and people well enough. Because of this, human judgment and effectuation will always be a key component to any reimagined process. For example, when Royal Dutch Shell sends its robots to monitor equipment and perform safety checks in its remote facility in Kazakhstan, it still requires the know-how of workers who are on the lookout for hazards. The robot, called Sensabot, is the first of its kind approved for use by oil and gas companies in potentially dangerous environments. A remote worker operates Sensabot, watching video feed and making judgments about risks.[11] Similarly, human expertise also remains a crucial component of reimagined processes at Caterpillar Inc. When a new assembly line is being designed there, engineers are needed to "walk" through an

AI-generated digital model of the line. The virtual walkthrough enables engineers to look for issues in the assembly, service, or ergonomics early on, finding potential problems before the line is built. This allows human experts to exercise their judgment to resolve any ambiguities or other issues early on in the process.

FUSION SKILL #4: *Intelligent Interrogation*

Definition: Knowing how best to ask questions of AI, across levels of abstraction, to get the insights you need.

How do you probe a massively complex system? How do you predict interactions between complex layers of data? People simply can't do this on their own, so they must ask questions of their friendly AI. "Twin, how certain are you?" "Twin, what do you recommend?" At GE, maintenance professionals who have the skill of intelligent interrogation understand the capabilities and limitations of the AI system and know how to get the information they need to make an informed decision. The workers play to strengths and don't duplicate the machine's strengths. In the process, the machine is training the humans in how to use it, just as the humans train the machine. In the end, it's human business and operational expertise that make the call for fixing or replacing a rotor, for instance.

In our research, we see intelligent interrogation at work in a range of areas. Workers intelligently interrogate when they optimize train freights and cargo, when they investigate drug compounds and molecular interactions, and when they try to find optimal retail pricing. Retail pricing, in particular, offers a useful scenario for intelligent interrogation thanks to the large complex data behind the scenes that can make or break sales.

Steve Schnur, who runs retail operations at a major resort, uses AI from Revionics to optimize prices in the convenience stores on-site. Even a small adjustment in the price of Advil or Band-Aids produces a significant effect—something that would have been impossible to understand (and ultimately control) without AI and an operator asking the AI system smart questions. Schnur's team uses the system to find the best prices of Advil, Band-Aids, soda, and more at any given time under any number of constraints, based on weekly sales reports on about seven thousand items. Schnur poses the question: "If you raise the price of Advil, what happens to Tylenol?" The system can figure out the relationship between Advil and Tylenol, even though they're only classified by stock-keeping units, and show that, for instance, the last time Advil was raised by twenty-five cents, sales of Tylenol increased. The system also lets Schnur probe pricing decisions in other ways, too, like "show me the most beneficial price changes" and "tell me which items will sell the least with a price increase." The smarter the questions, the more insight he can gain, and the better picture AI can paint for him of his overall operations.[12]

At GE, it's not just the turbines and rotors that are modeled by digital-twin software. The software is also modeling workers. By modeling workers' behaviors and interactions, the software itself can determine how to optimize its own performance. This results in user-friendly software and equipment that allow novice employees and new users to learn how to use them faster.

With all this digital guidance of work as it is performed, people might begin to offload too much expertise to the systems. Bill Ruh, CEO of GE Digital, is aware of this possibility and emphasizes the importance of human judgment and training that keeps skills from eroding. "You have to train people not to let the automation be their guide on everything—good human judgment comes into play," Ruh says. "I think the idea of human judgment being trained into people so that the automation doesn't become a crutch to what they do is really the difficult scenario we will be dealing with." Intelligent interrogation includes knowing when outputs don't make sense or that certain data inputs might be skewing results. "I think that we've got to be cognizant that the machine is not all powerful," Ruh says.[13]

FUSION SKILL #5: *Bot-based Empowerment*

Definition: Working well with AI agents to extend your capabilities, and create superpowers in business processes and professional careers.

Through bot-based empowerment, people can punch above their weight using intelligent agents at work. Imagine being a freelancer or contractor with a staff of employees at your beck and call, but your employees are digital bots, not people. The effect is that you can have the administrative and operational support that's more common for a CEO than a one-person show. Shivon Zilis, investor at Bloomberg Beta writes in a 2016 article: "Agents will make this possible, using a blend of learning algorithms and distributed labor to perform an ever-widening range of tasks at low cost. With help from these agents, we'll be able to look as smart as those CEOs do today." Zilis continues: "We'll also become more productive. Most knowledge workers spend less than half their time doing things they're really good at (i.e., what they've been hired to do). The rest is spent doing research, arranging meetings, coordinating with other people, and performing other minutia of office life. These tasks could easily be done just as well by a machine or intelligent service."[14]

Myriad bots are available to help people become better at their work. There are scheduling agents such as Clara and x.ai. There are tools to organize regular meetings so that you can mimic "chief of staff" activities with bots in Slack like Howdy, Standup Bot, Tatsu, and Geekbot. You can share meeting minutes and highlight keywords with tools like Gridspace Sift and Pogo. You can improve writing with Textio or IBM's Watson Tone Analyzer. And you can even have a bot post updates or pictures to social media to build your professional and personal brand on your behalf with Doli.io. (For a description of bot-based empowerment in job searches, see the sidebar "Leveraging AI to Find a Job.")

Even those at the top of the corporate ladder can use AI systems to punch above their weight. Marc Benioff, CEO of Salesforce, relies on his company's AI product Einstein Forecasting in regular meetings with his executive team. The platform is capable of performing sophisticated modeling and forecasting, allowing Benioff to cut more easily to the heart of the matter at hand. "For a CEO," he notes, "typically the way it works is you have various people in your staff meeting who are telling you what they want to tell you to get you to believe what they want you to believe. Einstein comes without bias." Benioff says he puts his trust in Einstein's objectivity, which has helped him to minimize the internal politics of his executive meetings and more accurately forecast sales. "To have Einstein guidance has transformed me as a CEO," he asserts.[15]

Of course, having the right tools is one thing; using them effectively is another. The problem is that not everyone possesses the skills necessary to assemble and deploy a portfolio of bots in the optimal ways to increase their effectiveness and productivity at work.

FUSION SKILL #6: *Holistic Melding*

Definition: The ability to develop robust mental models of AI agents to improve process outcomes.

The world's first robotic eye surgery was performed in 2016 at Oxford University's John Radcliffe Hospital. The patient, whose retina had been misshapen by an overgrown membrane, needed to have the membrane removed. That posed a challenge because it was only a hundredth of a millimeter thick, and a mistake would damage the retina. Normally, a surgeon would have to physically calm her heart rate to carefully make such precise incisions between beats. But with robotic surgery, the surgeon instead sat at a console, nudging a joystick. The robot's surgical tools, which are designed to eliminate jitter or tremulous movements, enabled the skilled operator to complete a surgery faster and with fewer complications than without.[16]

Robots are revolutionizing the field of surgery by allowing surgeons to reach hard-to-access organs, perform precise cuts, and suture at angles with previously impossible dexterity. But the key to the success of these surgeries remains the surgeons and their ability to learn the skills required to operate the robot—in essence, the ability to project their surgical skills into the body of a machine.

Holistic melding is known to anyone who's used a tool that's felt so familiar that it was as if the tool were an extension of his or her own body or mind. Melding occurs when you parallel park your car without assistance (you seem to *just know* how far the trunk juts out) or swing a tennis racket to make contact with a ball. Increasingly, machines are getting better at melding with us as well. When you start typing search terms, Google not only

Leveraging AI to Find a Job

Bot-based empowerment skills also come in handy for job searches. If there's one guarantee for workers in these AI days, it's that the job landscape is quickly changing. Positions such as data scientist, which barely existed five years ago, are now all the rage. And positions that focus on rote tasks like data entry are quickly fading from job listings. How can people forge new career paths, find new training opportunities, or boost their online presence or personal brand on social media? The answer is bot-based empowerment.

Jobs searches and recruitment is often a numbers game, so you're already behind if you haven't automated various elements of this process through services like LinkedIn or up-and-coming AI-based job-search assistants like Wade & Wendy or Ella.

By early 2017, LinkedIn had made it easy for people to apply for potential jobs with one click. The company had also made it simple for recruiters to blast messages to qualified potential employees. At the same time, services like Wade & Wendy and Ella offer a wholly different job search experience that starts with the interface: a conversational AI chatbot. Wade, for instance, works with people on their behalf to find jobs that fit their interests, skills, and background. Wendy is the HR counterpart that automates recruiting for the right candidate.[a] Similarly, Ella is also a chatbot that asks questions about skills and desired

a. Kayla Matthews, "5 Chatbots That Will Help You Find a Job," *Venture Beat*, June 22, 2017, https://venturebeat.com/2017/06/22/5-chatbots-that-will-help-you -find-a-job/.

job titles. Ella then searches for jobs, including those that aren't publicly posted. The AI refines searches over time so that the results are more targeted. Sean Paley, senior vice president of digital innovation at Lee Hecht Harrison, explains the benefits of services like Wade & Wendy and Ella: "By automating the process of wading through tons of data, individuals will be able to focus on more complex and personalized components of a job search, such as interview preparation with a career coach and networking."[b] Bot-based empowerment is a prime example of a skill that allows people to focus more on the human side of the job hunt.

It can also help people tell a more coherent story about their career. Product marketer Esther Crawford was looking for a better way to market herself. Her bot, EstherBot, automatically answers questions about career history, education, and even hobbies that recruiters might ask. "I wanted to use a bot," said Crawford, "to tell the story of how I got from having a master's in international relations to being a product manager for startups."[c] For people with bot-based empowerment skills, they know how and when to deploy AI agents like EstherBot, and they are able to effectively manage a small army of such bots.

b. "Lee Hecht Harrison Introduces Ella-the Career Transition Industry's First AI-Powered Digital Career Agent," *PR Newswire*, February 8, 2017, https://www .prnewswire.com/news-releases/lee-hecht-harrison-introduces-ella-the-career -transition-industrys-first-ai-powered-digital-career-agent-300403757.html.

c. Steven Melendez, "What It's Like to Use a Chatbot to Apply for Jobs," *Fast-Company*, April 27, 2016, https://www.fastcompany.com/3059265/what-its -like-to-use-a-chatbot-to-apply-for-jobs.

considers the most generally popular associations for its auto-complete feature, but also considers your geographic location, previous search terms, and other factors. It can feel as if the software is reading your thoughts.

In the age of human-machine fusion, holistic (physical and mental) melding will become increasingly important. The full reimagination of business processes only becomes possible when humans create working mental models of how machines work and learn, and when machines capture user-behavior data to update their interactions. With melding, processes become flexible, adaptable, and potentially fun, akin perhaps to dancing with a skilled partner, switching from time to time the roles of lead and follow.

A Canadian startup called Kindred AI is hoping that melding can help train its robots to perform dexterous tasks at ultra-fast speeds. It's pairing its systems with human "pilots" in virtual reality headsets, who hold motion-sensing gadgets; their movement information is transmitted directly to the robots.[17] In BMW factories, where human workers already share the floor with cobots, both people and machine actively sense their environments and have learned how best to orchestrate each other's respective movements. The robots in these scenarios act as extensions of the workers' own bodies.

There is no single way to facilitate melding between humans and machines, which makes the job of the manager and CEO in some ways more difficult. Approaches will likely depend on a specific team's needs and require a trial-and-error approach. One example of the diversity of approaches, though, can be found within the robot-human teams that operate NASA's Mars Exploration Rovers. On these teams, people program a robot to complete its tasks within the constraints of equipment, power, time, onboard memory, and instrumentation. According to Princeton ethnographer Janet Vertesi, to make decisions for how a robot completes its activities, the team must "decide how to decide." In effect, they come up with their own organization, codes of conduct, and rules of governing, she writes.[18]

FUSION SKILL #7: *Reciprocal Apprenticing*

Definition: (1) Performing tasks alongside AI agents so they can learn new skills; (2) on-the-job training for people so they can work well within AI-enhanced processes.

IPsoft's natural-language AI assistant called Amelia tackles roles as diverse as IT help-desk agent, mortgage broker, and expert question-answerer for a British town council's website and call center. How can a single software program do so much? Human experts train Amelia, both explicitly and implicitly, how to do its jobs. Only through apprenticing can AI like Amelia or Microsoft's Cortana succeed in so many different contexts; future work will require a keen understanding of the dynamics inherent in human-machine apprenticeships.

For instance, if machine apprenticing is implemented in a sneaky way, where employees don't explicitly know that some or all of their work is being used to train machines, both machines and management can generate distrust. In the best-case scenarios, though, apprenticing can act as a salve against anxiety, passivity, and a sense of helplessness in human-machine interactions. Give people some level of control, make them feel invested in the future performance of a system or process, and they'll see AI as a colleague rather than a foe.

Apprenticing as a fusion skill marks a distinct break from the way we've historically managed technology. Traditionally, technological education has gone in one direction: people have learned how to use machines. But with AI, machines are learning from humans, and humans, in turn, learn again from machines. Apprenticing means customer service representatives or anyone who's working in conjunction with an AI agent will act as "role models" to their digital colleagues. Role modeling, of course, requires the teacher to have appropriate technical skills; it also requires building AI in such a way that it's easily trainable; interfaces matter in human-machine apprenticeships.

Amelia, for instance, uses an interface that, behind the scenes, observes and watches the digital behavior of its human operators—a kind of background learning. Beyond background learning, software facilitates the apprenticeship relationship by escalating questions it can't answer to a human colleague, all the while observing how the problem is solved. Whereas traditional automation capital degrades over time, intelligent automation assets constantly improve.[19]

Of course, in fusion relationships, not only the machines need to be trained. AI is bringing about a renaissance in human apprenticeships. In fact, apprenticeships for people will be critical in filling the aforementioned skills gap in manufacturing, which is accelerating due to intelligent automation. Formal, government-backed programs like the one funded by the Apprenticeship Levy in the UK will be a test. Firms with a payroll of more than £3 million will have to pay a small tax, which they will be able to recoup (in addition to £15,000 and a 10 percent bonus for each £1 paid into the pot) if they use the money to buy accredited apprenticeship training. That is, they can have the money back and more, if they hire unskilled workers and train them. The challenge, of course, will be developing apprenticeship training, which will likely need to vary across industries and even from firm to firm.

So, ultimately, each organization must fine-tune apprenticeship programs that are right for it. The CIO at a financial technology firm notes that AI upset personnel roles within a team. But through reimagining, the bank was able to find an apprenticeship arrangement that made sense for workers, machines, and management. "Because the bank started to hire professionals with different skills and experience (e.g., data management, data science, programming, and analytics) to manage the system, the role of more senior members of the loans team became one of training and supporting the new recruits on the loans industry and providing the industry context for their roles. Their role also became integral in teaching the AI algorithm to learn effectively," the CIO says.

This experience with apprenticeships demonstrates something more fundamental about work in the age of human-machine hybrids: one of the most important characteristics, for a human worker or a machine, is not necessarily to have the exact skill for a job but be able to learn. "Don't be a know-it-all," says Microsoft CEO Satya Nadella on the topic. "Be a learn-it-all."[20]

FUSION SKILL #8: *Relentless Reimagining*

Definition: The rigorous discipline of creating new processes and business models from scratch, rather than simply automating old processes.

The final—and perhaps most important—hybrid skill is the ability to reimagine how things currently are. In essence, this is what this book has been all about—reimagining how AI can transform and improve work, organizational processes, business models, and even entire industries.

As we mentioned in the part two introduction, Stitch Fix is reimagining the online sales and order-fulfillment processes. Similarly, Capital One is known for its aggressive and relentless use of AI, cloud computing, big data, and open-source technology, and it has scored a number of significant victories. It was, for example, the first in the industry to launch capability on Amazon's Alexa, enabling customers to check their balances, pay bills, and perform other transactions on that platform. More recently, it became the first among competitors to introduce its own intelligent customer-facing chatbot. Named Eno, the technology is equipped with natural-language processing to handle smartphone text conversations with customers. A related application deploys machine learning to alert account holders to unusual transactions that might indicate fraud.

To maintain its AI edge, Capital One has recently established a machine-learning Center of Excellence (COE) for studying how the technology can be used to reimagine the customer experience. Staffed with employees from the company's offices in New York, Virginia, and Washington, DC, the COE will be looking at how AI might be applied to help customers manage their spending better. The center will also be investigating the creation of computer programs that will help explain how an AI system arrived at the decisions it makes. "The goal is to make Capital One a preeminent machine-learning company," says Wenchel.[21]

Capital One is moving beyond being a financial services firm; it's becoming a technology company. "We're in a business where two of our biggest products are software and data," notes Rob Alexander, CIO of the company. And that transformation, according to Alexander, has led to fundamental changes at the company: "It requires a different talent base, and it requires a different mindset and an entirely different operating model."[22]

The organizational changes to help move Capital One into this new era of AI have also been significant. As just one example, the company now deploys technology teams that embrace some of the principles of agile software development, in which the goal is to fail fast in order to succeed quickly. The management philosophy of "test and learn" is a core principle in Capital One's culture. In late 2014, the company established the "Garage," an innovation center on its Plano, Texas, campus. (The name "Garage" refers to the humble origins of many start-ups in Silicon Valley.) At the center, staffers aren't given any specific orders, just general guidance to "massively improve our consumers' experience with our product."[23]

That type of commitment to relentlessly reimagining processes, employee roles and skill sets, and the core business itself is common among companies that are leaders in deploying advanced AI technologies.

In essence, reimagining is a fundamental skill that lays the foundation for the other skills like intelligent interrogating and bot-based empowerment. It is this capability to reimagine that enables people to more easily adapt to a different everyday world, in which advanced AI technologies are continually transforming organizational processes, business models, and industries.

Opportunities in Neural Opportunism

The concept of fusion skills—abilities for combining the relative strengths of a human and machine to create a better outcome than either could alone—aligns well with research from cognitive science. Neural opportunism—the idea that people naturally use technologies to augment themselves—as well as ideas of extended intelligence and embodied intelligence are relevant here. Humans, as research has shown, incorporate tools and technologies as part of our own cognition.[24] From eyeglasses to bicycles to fighter jets, these tools, when we use them often enough and at an expert level, can feel like extensions of our bodies and minds. Artificial intelligence brings another dimension to this kind of bio-technical symbiosis: smart machines are themselves neurally opportunistic with regard to their own unique strengths. By design, they collect information about their surroundings and incorporate it into their own cognition. So these eight skills, the "S" part of MELDS, put emphasis on a new kind of relational competence that's rarely if ever discussed in today's economic analyses or corporate talent development programs. Fusion skills require a novel way of thinking about human expertise and, by extension, a very different approach to educating and retraining the workforce.

Creating Your Future in the Human + Machine Era

Whwhen it comes to discussions about artificial intelligence, much of the conversation tends to focus on job displacement and fear that computers will one day take over the world. The underlying assumption is that humans and machines are competitors, and that AI systems, with their superior speed, processing power, and stamina in so many contexts, will directly replace us in companies—and perhaps even outside the workplace as well.

A number of quantitative economic studies have only heightened those fears. As one study concluded, "absent appropriate fiscal policy that redistributes from winners to losers, smart machines can mean long-term misery for all."[1] But such quantitative studies have typically focused on broad industry trends, and in doing so they have missed what's been happening behind the scenes in everyday processes and practices.

From our own research—including observational and case analysis across 450 organizations within our sample of 1,500— we were able to identify a number of important phenomena that the quantitative surveys have failed to capture. One is the concept of "fusion skills": humans and machines coming together to form new kinds of jobs and work experiences. This forms the "missing middle" that has been absent in much of today's polarizing jobs debate that has pitted humans on one side and machines on the other. And it's within this missing middle that leading-edge companies have been reimagining their work processes, achieving outsize improvements in performance. To obtain such results, though, executives must lead their organizations through the transformation by making the necessary investments, including retraining workers to fill those missing-middle roles.

Doing Different Things, and Doing Things Differently

To extrapolate how companies will be making the transition to a new era of human + machine, we first needed to understand how executives are deploying AI in their businesses today. In part one of this book we described various applications in manufacturing and supply chain (chapter 1), back-office operations (chapter 2), R&D and business innovation (chapter 3), and marketing, sales, and customer service (chapter 4). Studying those applications gave us a clear view of the future, enabling us to identify the different ways in which companies were filling the missing middle by creating new, enhanced jobs that have cracked open novel economic and employment opportunities.

Specifically, our research discovered just how different these new jobs were from traditional kinds of work. Already, today, 61% of activities in the missing middle require employees to do *different things* and to do *things differently*—hence the crucial need for companies to reimagine their processes and reskill their employees. As we discussed in chapter 5, these *different things* include training data models, or explaining and responsibly sustaining an AI system's performance. And, as we described in chapter 6, these new jobs also include employees doing *things differently* using amplification, interaction, and embodiment to get a job done with superhuman performance. Rather than relying on economic data far removed from organizational practice, you must observe these differences directly to understand and appreciate them.

So far, though, only a small number of companies we've surveyed have begun to capture the potential of fusion skills, and in doing so they have been able to reimagine their businesses, operating models, and processes in innovative ways. These firms—General Electric, Microsoft, BMW, Google, Amazon, and others—recognize that AI isn't your typical capital investment; its value actually increases over time and it, in turn, improves the value of people as well. Indeed, when humans and machines are allowed to do what each does best, the result is a virtuous cycle of enhanced work that leads to productivity boosts, increased worker satisfaction, and greater innovation. As such, these companies are leading their industries with redesigned job descriptions and learning and retraining programs, all sustained by a new set of leadership practices (described in chapter 7). Their early successes have proven that they're on the right path.

The pressing issue, though, is that most organizations have been slow in filling the missing middle, and the results have begun to show. In the United States, 6 million jobs remain open, and within this group, more than 350,000 manufacturing jobs go unfilled each month due to a lack of qualified workers.[2] Globally, across the twelve largest economies by GDP, 38 percent of employers report difficulty filling jobs.[3] The problem right now isn't so much that robots are replacing jobs; it's that workers aren't prepared with the right skills necessary for jobs that are evolving fast due to new technologies, such as AI. And the challenge will only grow as companies apply AI and reimagine work in other areas. For example, the largest one hundred global employers report that more than one-third of skill sets that aren't yet crucial today will be by 2020.[4]

There is a skills gap on the digital side of manufacturing, too. As factories become increasingly high tech, they require more workers with software smarts. Siemens, for example, has recognized this and plans to hire seven thousand more people by 2020 in positions related to training and using collaborative robotics, software engineering, and computer science. But these sorts of positions wouldn't be included in traditional reports of the job outlook in the AI era, as AI has blurred the lines between blue and white collar, new and old jobs. "People may not count those jobs in IT and software development as manufacturing jobs," says Eric Spiegel, the company's US CEO, "but they really are related to manufacturing."[5]

Our research has found that the real issue isn't simply that humans will be replaced by machines; it's that humans need to be better prepared to fill the growing number of jobs in the missing middle. In chapter 8, we described in detail the kinds of fusion skills that have become increasingly important in this new era of human-machine collaboration. And we discussed the importance of "neural opportunism," as people will increasingly need to incorporate AI tools to extend the capabilities of their bodies and minds.

Unfortunately, there is not much evidence that business or political leaders are making the necessary investments in these areas. In the United States, the 2016 White House report "Artificial Intelligence, Automation, and the Economy" notes that the nation spends only around 0.1 percent of its GDP on programs that help people adjust to workplace changes. This number has fallen over the last thirty years, and the federal readjustment programs that exist—mostly used to help people deal with coal mines or military bases that close—are not designed to help people whose jobs are lost or changed by automation.[6] Results are mixed in other countries. Japan and China are among those that stand out by making significant commitments to AI education and workforce training as the core piece of long-term national AI strategies. For instance, China's State Council has the stated goal of making the nation equal among leading AI countries by 2020 and the world's "premier artificial intelligence innovation center by 2030."[7] This development plan includes major investments in retraining workers for an economy where "collaboration between humans and machines will become a mainstream production and service mode."[8]

A Call to Action: Reimagining Business

AI is rapidly making inroads in business. Its swift adoption means that questions on both the opportunities and risks are at the forefront of most discussions. Leaders are faced with decisions today that have profound consequences. It's here, in the practical application of AI to business, where we hope this book can offer the most help.

For years, the dream of many researchers was to create an artificial intelligence that could rival that of people. However, we're seeing that AI is instead becoming a tool to extend our own human capabilities. In turn, we're guiding AI systems to evolve into better tools that further extend our capabilities. Never before in history have our tools been so responsive to us, and we to our tools. As we see with fusion skills and the missing middle, the real opportunity is to make work more human, reimagine business with a more human approach, and equip people with superhuman capabilities to perform more effectively.

We believe our perspective, grounded in people and machines working together, requires a new approach and calls for the reimagination of businesses and our business processes. AI is enabling business leaders to understand better than ever what their customers and employees need. Through AI and processes built around hybrid human-machine capabilities, organizations can take these needs into account, realizing solutions that benefit both business and people.

Our primary goal in *Human + Machine* is to provide leaders, managers, and workers with the necessary tools to prepare for this coming third wave of process transformation. As we've discussed throughout these chapters, this era calls for humans and machines to fill the missing middle by working closely together in new types of roles with a new kind of collaborative partnership. To enable that, we have described how executives must implement organizational changes to support a culture that encourages the reimagining of work process, all while investing in learning platforms and the continual retraining of employees. This obviously applies to the underlying fusion skills necessary to develop, maintain, and manage AI-enabled business capabilities, but it's also pertinent to other softer skills, such as those required to make difficult ethical decisions regarding the technology.

As our MELDS approach shows, successful implementations of AI require more than attention to the technology itself. The fundamental focus of the leadership component of MELDS is to always keep people at the center of any AI initiative, taking into account employees and customers, as well as other human stakeholders. For example, as AI is introduced into the workplace, executives need to assess the various implications: How will job requirements need to evolve, and how will any labor displacements be balanced with broader workforce considerations? What new investments in talent are needed to retain industry expertise, and which employees may need to be counseled and retrained?

There are also government regulations, ethical design standards (such as those proposed by the IEEE), and prevailing public sentiment to consider. As we've discussed, it's incumbent on companies to ensure that the AI systems they deploy aren't biased, and they need to be able to understand and explain why they made certain decisions. Executives and managers must also know which decisions are being delegated solely to machines (versus which decisions require human intervention), and there must be accountability for that process. In certain cases, transparency of the entire decision-making process might be necessary.

Lastly, firms must proactively keep maturing AI technology in line with new laws and regional policies, such as the General Data Protection Regulation (GDPR) in Europe. In particular, personal data will require special attention in different ways in different regions, especially as AI systems become increasingly capable of deriving unprecedented types of insights beyond basic demographics.

The above issues are of crucial importance, and the fate of many people, firms, industries, and countries will depend on the solutions that are chosen. As we reimagine business and our organizations through AI, there is tremendous potential to create a better future and improve the way the world works and lives; to not only increase business performance, but to implement more sustainable solutions that better utilize critical resources on the planet, and drive powerful new services and forms of interaction with consumers and workers.

In our research, we found that companies that use AI to augment their human talent while reimagining their business processes achieve step gains in performance, propelling themselves to the forefront of their industries. Firms that continue deploying AI merely to automate in a traditional fashion may see some performance benefits, but those improvements will eventually stall. We predict that within the next decade, there will emerge a vast difference between the winners and losers, a difference determined not on whether an organization has implemented AI, but on *how* it's done it.

And that's where the human element truly comes in. As we've shown, AI gives people powerful tools to do more, in essence to perform with superhuman capability. In doing so, AI has the potential to rehumanize work, giving us more time to be human, rather than using our time to work like machines.

We're at the cusp of a new era of business transformation, the age of AI, and our actions today have great bearing on how the future unfolds. We hope our book has provided you with a better lens to understand the opportunities and challenges ahead, and a road map for applying AI in the work that you do. Through the responsible application of AI and the relentless reimagining of work, people can and should reap the benefits of intelligent machines. As we take these steps, it's time to discard dusty old notions of humans versus machines, and instead embrace an exciting new world of human *and* machine.

Our Commitment to Skills for the Age of AI

Our goal with *Human + Machine* is to help people navigate the changes that AI is bringing to business, government, and the economy. We strongly believe that artificial intelligence, guided by the right management approach, will yield innovations that truly improve the way the world works and lives. This will also generate a wealth of new types of jobs in the missing middle.

However, we also recognize that AI will bring dislocation, disruption, and challenges to many. It is essential that we provide *all* people with the education, training, and support they need to take on the many jobs required in the missing middle. In support of this imperative, we are *donating our net royalties* from the sale of this book *to fund education and retraining programs* focused on helping people develop the fusion skills they need to be a part of the age of AI.

NOTES

Introduction

1. DPCcars, "BMW Factory Humans & Robots Work Together at Dingolfing Plant," YouTube video, 25:22 minutes, Posted March 2, 2017, https://www.youtube.com/watch?v=Dm3Nyb2lCvs.

2. Robert J. Thomas, Alex Kass, and Ladan Davarzani, "Recombination at Rio Tinto: Mining at the Push of a Button," Accenture, Sept 2, 2015, www.accenture.com/t20150902T013400_w_/us-en_acnmedia/Accenture/Conversion-Assets/DotCom/Documents/Global/PDF/Dualpub_21/Accenture-Impact-Of-Tech-Rio-Tinto.pdf.

Chapter 1

1. Nikolaus Correll, "How Investing in Robots Actually Helps Human Jobs," *Time*, April 2, 2017, http://time.com/4721687/investing-robots-help-human-jobs/.

2. Will Knight, "This Factory Robot Learns a New Job Overnight," *MIT Technology Review*, March 18, 2016, https://www.technologyreview.com/s/601045/this-factory-robot-learns-a-new-job-overnight/; Pavel Alpeyev, "Zero to Expert in Eight Hours: These Robots Can Learn for Themselves," *Bloomberg*, December 3, 2015, https://www.bloomberg.com/news/articles/2015-12-03/zero-to-expert-in-eight-hours-these-robots-can-learn-for-themselves.

3. Knight, "This Factory Robot Learns a New Job Overnight."

4. "Company Information: History of iRobot," http://www.irobot.com /About-iRobot/Company-Information/History.aspx, accessed November 2, 2017.

5. H. James Wilson, Allan Alter, and Sharad Sachdev, "Business Processes Are Learning to Hack Themselves," *Harvard Business Review*, June 27, 2016, https://hbr.org/2016/06/business-processes-are-learning-to-hack -themselves; author interview with Andreas Nettsträter, February 8, 2016.

6. Steve Lohr, "G.E., the 124-Year-Old Software Start-Up," *New York Times*, August 27, 2016, https://www.nytimes.com/2016/08/28/technology /ge-the-124-year-old-software-start-up.html.

7. Charles Babcock, "GE Doubles Down on 'Digital Twins' for Business Knowledge," *Information Week*, October 24, 2016, http://www .informationweek.com/cloud/software-as-a-service/ge-doubles-down -on-digital-twins-for-business-knowledge/d/d-id/1327256.

8. Ibid.

9. Tomas Kellner, "Wind in the Cloud? How the Digital Wind Farm Will Make Wind Power 20 Percent More Efficient," GE Reports, September 27, 2015, http://www.gereports.com/post/119300678660/wind-in-the -cloud-how-the-digital-wind-farm-will/.

10. Author interview with Joe Caracappa, October 13, 2016.

11. Leanna Garfield, "Inside the World's Largest Vertical Farm, Where Plants Stack 30 Feet High," *Business Insider*, March 15, 2016, http:// www.businessinsider.com/inside-aerofarms-the-worlds-largest-vertical -farm-2016-3.

12. "Digital Agriculture: Improving Profitability," Accenture, https:// www.accenture.com/us-en/insight-accenture-digital-agriculture-solutions.

Chapter 2

1. Jordan Etkin and Cassie Mogilner, "Does Variety Increase Happiness?" *Advances in Consumer Research* 42 (2014):53–58.

2. Author interview with Andrew Anderson, CEO of Celaton, September 29, 2016.

3. Richard Feloni, "Consumer-Goods Giant Unilever Has Been Hiring Employees Using Brain Games and Artificial Intelligence—And It's a Huge Success," *Business Insider*, June 28, 2017, www.businessinsider.com /unilever-artificial-intelligence-hiring-process-2017-6.

4. Author interview with Roger Dickey, Founder of Gigster, November 21, 2016.

5. "IPsoft's Cognitive Agent Amelia Takes on Pioneering Role in Bank with SEB," IPsoft press release, October 6, 2016, http://www.ipsoft .com/2016/10/06/ipsofts-cognitive-agent-amelia-takes-on-pioneering-role -in-banking-with-seb/.

6. Sage Lazzaro, "Meet Aida, the AI Banker That NEVER Takes a Day Off: Swedish Firm Reveals Robot Customer Service Rep It Says Is 'Always at Work, 24/7, 365 Days a Year,'" *Daily Mail UK*, July 31, 2017, http://www .dailymail.co.uk/sciencetech/article-4748090/Meet-Aida-AI-robot-banker-s -work.html.

7. "Darktrace Antigena Launched: New Era as Cyber AI Fights Back," Darktrace press release, April 4, 2017, https://www.darktrace.com /press/2017/158/.

8. Linda Musthaler, "Vectra Networks Correlates Odd Bits of User Behavior That Signal an Attack in Progress," *Network World*, January 9, 2015, https://www.networkworld.com/article/2867009/network-security /vectra-networks-correlates-odd-bits-of-user-behavior-that-signal-an -attack-in-progress.html.

Chapter 3

1. Bill Vlasic, "G.M. Takes a Back Seat to Tesla as America's Most Valued Carmaker," *New York Times*, April 10, 2017, https://www.nytimes .com/2017/04/10/business/general-motors-stock-valuation.html.

2. "All Tesla Cars Being Produced Now Have Full Self-Driving Hardware," Tesla press release, October 19, 2016, https://www.tesla.com/blog /all-tesla-cars-being-produced-now-have-full-self-driving-hardware.

3. Isaac Asimov, *Fantastic Voyage II: Destination Brain* (New York: Doubleday, 1987), 276–277.

4. Arif E. Jinha, "Article 50 Million: An Estimate of the Number of Scholarly Journals in Existence," *Learned Publishing* 23, no. 1 (July 2010): 258–263.

5. Author interview with Shivon Zilis, January 31, 2017.

6. Author interview with Colin Hill, CEO of GNS Healthcare, February 12, 2016.

7. Ibid.

8. Margaret Rhodes, "Check Out Nike's Crazy New Machine-Designed Track Shoe," *Wired*, July 20, 2016, https://www.wired .com/2016/07/check-nikes-crazy-new-machine-designed-track-shoe/.

9. Author interview with Scott Clark, CEO of SigOpt, November 22, 2016.

10. Author interview with Colin Hill, CEO of GNS Healthcare, February 12, 2016.

11. Author interview with Brandon Allgood, CTO of Numerate, July 7, 2016.

12. Ibid.

Chapter 4

1. Phil Wainewright, "Salesforce Captures the Limits of AI in a Coca-Cola Cooler," *Diginomica*, March 7, 2017, http://diginomica .com/2017/03/07/salesforce-captures-the-limits-of-ai-in-a-coca-cola-cooler/.

2. "Transitioning to a Circular Economy," Philips, https://www.usa .philips.com/c-dam/corporate/about-philips-n/sustainability/sustainabilitypdf /philips-circular-economy.pdf.

3. Jordan Crook, "Oak Labs, with $41M in Seed, Launches a Smart Fitting Room Mirror," *TechCrunch*, November 18, 2015, https://techcrunch .com/2015/11/18/oak-labs-with-4-1m-in-seed-launches-a-smart-fitting -room-mirror/.

4. "The Race for Relevance, Total Retail 2016: United States," PwC, February 2016, http://www.pwc.com/us/en/retail-consumer/publications /assets/total-retail-us-report.pdf.

5. "Staffing Is Difficult," Percolata, http://www.percolata.com/customers /staffing-is-difficult, accessed October 24, 2017.

6. "Bionic Mannequins Are Watching You," *Retail Innovation*, April 2, 2013, http://retail-innovation.com/bionic-mannequins-are-watching -you; and Cotton Timberlake, Chiara Remondini and Tommaso Ebhardt, "Mannequins Collect Data on Shoppers Via Facial-Recognition Software," *Washington Post*, November 22, 2012.

7. H. James Wilson, Narendra Mulani, and Allan Alter, "Sales Gets a Machine-Learning Makeover," *MIT Sloan Management Review*, May 17, 2016, sloanreview.mit.edu/article/sales-gets-a-machine-learning-makeover/.

8. Pierre Nanterme and Paul Daugherty, "2017 Technology Vision Report," Accenture, https://www.accenture.com/t20170125T084845__w__ /us-en/_acnmedia/Accenture/next-gen-4/tech-vision-2017/pdf/Accenture -TV17-Full.pdf?la=en.

9. A. S. Miner et al. "Smartphone-Based Conversational Agents and Responses to Questions about Mental Health, Interpersonal Violence, and physical Health," *JAMA Internal Medicine* 176, no. 5 (May 2016): 619–625.

Notes

10. Mark Wilson, "This Startup Is Teaching Chatbots Real Empathy," *FastCompany*, August 8, 2016, https://www.fastcodesign.com/3062546/this -startup-is-teaching-chatbots-real-empathy.

11. Ibid.

12. Laura Beckstead, Daniel Hayden, and Curtis Schroeder, "A Picture's Worth A Thousand Words . . . and Maybe More," *Forbes*, August 5, 2016, https://www.forbes.com/sites/oracle/2016/08/05/a-pictures-worth-a -thousand-words-and-maybe-more/.

Part Two Introduction

1. Robert J. Thomas, Alex Kass, and Ladan Davarzani, "Recombination at Rio Tinto: Mining at the Push of a Button," Accenture, Sept 2, 2015, www.accenture.com/t20150902T013400__w__/us-en_acnmedia /Accenture/Conversion-Assets/DotCom/Documents/Global/PDF/ Dualpub_21/Accenture-Impact-Of-Tech-Rio-Tinto.pdf.

2. James Wilson, "Rio Tinto's Driverless Trains Are Running Late," *Financial Times*, April 19, 2016, https://www.ft.com/content/fe27fd68-0630 -11e6-9b51-0fb5e65703ce.

3. H. James Wilson, Paul Daugherty and Prashant Shukla, "How One Clothing Company Blends AI and Human Expertise," *Harvard Business Review*, November 21, 2016, https://hbr.org/2016/11/how-one-clothing -company-blends-ai-and-human-expertise.

Chapter 5

1. Melissa Cefkin, "Nissan Anthropologist: We Need a Universal Language for Autonomous Cars," *2025AD*, January 27, 2017, https://www.2025ad.com /latest/nissan-melissa-cefkin-driverless-cars/.

2. Kim Tingley, "Learning to Love Our Robot Co-Workers," *New York Times*, February 23, 2017, https://www.nytimes.com/2017/02/23/magazine /learning-to-love-our-robot-co-workers.html.

3. Rossano Schifanella, Paloma de Juan, Liangliang Cao and Joel Tetreault, "Detecting Sacarsm in Multimodal Social Platforms," August 8, 2016, https://arxiv.org/pdf/1608.02289.

4. Elizabeth Dwoskin, "The Next Hot Job in Silicon Valley Is for Poets," *Washington Post*, April 7, 2016, https://www.washingtonpost.com /news/the-switch/wp/2016/04/07/why-poets-are-flocking-to-silicon-valley.

5. "Init.ai Case Study," Mighty AI, https://mty.ai/customers/init-ai/, accessed October 25, 2017.

6. Matt Burgess, "DeepMind's AI Has Learnt to Become 'Highly Aggressive" When It Feels Like It's Going to Lose," *Wired*, February 9, 2017, www.wired.co.uk/article/artificial-intelligence-social-impact-deepmind.

7. Paul X. McCarthy, "Your Garbage Data Is a Gold Mine," *Fast Company*, August 24, 2016, https://www.fastcompany.com/3063110/the-rise-of -weird-data.

8. John Lippert, "ZestFinance Issues Small, High-Rate Loans, Uses Big Data to Weed Out Deadbeats," *Washington Post*, October 11, 2014, https://www.washingtonpost.com/business/zestfinance-issues-small-high -rate-loans-uses-big-data-to-weed-out-deadbeats/2014/10/10/e34986b6 -4d71-11e4-aa5e-7153e466a02d_story.html.

9. Jenna Burrell, "How the Machine 'Thinks': Understanding Opacity in Machine Learning Algorithms," *Big Data & Society* (January–June 2016): 1–12, http://journals.sagepub.com/doi/abs/10.1177/2053951715622512.

10. Ibid.

11. Kim Tingley, "Learning to Love Our Robot Co-Workers," *New York Times*, February 23, 2017, https://www.nytimes.com/2017/02/23/magazine /learning-to-love-our-robot-co-workers.html.

12. Isaac Asimov, "Runaround," *Astounding Science Fiction* (March 1942).

13. Accenture Research Survey, January 2016.

14. Vyacheslav Polonski, "Would You Let an Algorithm Choose the Next US President?" World Economic Forum, November 1, 2016, https://www.weforum.org/agenda/2016/11/would-you-let-an-algorithm -choose-the-next-us-president/.

15. Mark O. Riedl and Brent Harrison, "Using Stories to Teach Human Values to Artificial Agents," in 2nd International Workshop on AI, Ethics, and Society, Association for the Advancement of Artificial Intelligence (2015), https://www.cc.gatech.edu/~riedl/pubs/aaai-ethics16.pdf.

16. Masahiro Mori, translated by Karl F. MacDorman and Norri Kageki, "The Uncanny Valley," *IEEE Spectrum*, June 12, 2012, https:// spectrum.ieee.org/automaton/robotics/humanoids/the-uncanny-valley.

Chapter 6

1. Margaret Rhodes, "So. Algorithms Are Designing Chairs Now," *Wired*, October 3, 2016, https://www.wired.com/2016/10/elbo-chair -autodesk-algorithm/.

2. Dan Howarth, "Generative Design Software Will Give Designers 'Superpowers,'" *Dezeen*, February 6, 2017, https://www.dezeen.com/2017/02/06 /generative-design-software-will-give-designers-superpowers-autodesk -university/.

3. "Illumeo: Changing How We See, Seek and Share Clinical Information," Philips, http://www.usa.philips.com/healthcare/product /HC881040/illumeo.

4. "Upskill Raises Series B Funding from Boeing and GE Ventures," Upskill.io press release, April 5, 2017, https://upskill.io/upskill-raises-series -b-funding-from-boeing-ventures-and-ge-ventures/.

5. Nicolas Moch and Michael Krigsman, "Customer Service with Amelia AI at SEB Bank," *CXO Talk*, August 15, 2017, https://www.cxotalk .com/video/customer-service-amelia-ai-seb-bank.

6. Peggy Hollinger, "Meet the Cobots: Humans and Robots Together on the factory floor," *Financial Times*, May 4, 2016, https://www.ft.com /content/6d5d609e-02e2-11e6-af1d-c47326021344?mhq5j=e6.

7. Will Knight, "How Human-Robot Teamwork Will Upend Manufacturing," *MIT Technology Review*, September 16, 2014, https://www .technologyreview.com/s/530696/how-human-robot-teamwork-will -upend-manufacturing/.

8. AutomotoTV, "Mercedes-Benz Industrie 4.0 More flexibility – Human Robot Cooperation (HRC)," YouTube video, 2:38 minutes, November 25, 2015, https://youtu.be/ZjaePUZPzug.

9. Peggy Hollinger, "Meet the Cobots: Humans and Robots Together on the Factory Floor," *Financial Times*, May 4, 2016, https://www.ft.com /content/6d5d609e-02e2-11e6-af1d-c47326021344?mhq5j=e6.

10. Interview with Richard Morris, Vice President of Assembly and Logistics, BWW Manufacturing Company, accessed at Advanced Motion Systems, Inc. "Universal Robots on BMW Assembly Line – ASME," YouTube video, April 7, 2014, https://WWW.youtube.com/watch?v= CROBmw5Txl.

11. Michael Reilly, "Rethink's Sawyer Robot Just Got a Whole Lot Smarter," *MIT Technology Review*, February 8, 2017, https://www.technologyreview .com/s/603608/rethinks-sawyer-robot-just-got-a-whole-lot-smarter/.

12. Cassie Werber, "The World's First Commercial Drone Delivery Service Has Launched in Rwanda," *Quartz*, October 14, 2016, https:// qz.com/809576/zipline-has-launched-the-worlds-first-commercial-drone -delivery-service-to-supply-blood-in-rwanda/.

13. Jessica Leber, "Doctors Without Borders Is Experimenting with Delivery Drones to Battle an Epidemic," *Fast Company*, October 16, 2014, https://www.fastcompany.com/3037013/doctors-without-borders-is -experimenting-with-delivery-drones-to-battle-an-epidemic.

14. Wings For Aid website, https://www.wingsforaid.org, accessed October 25, 2017.

Chapter 7

1. Shoshana Zuboff, *In the Age of the Smart Machine: The Future of Work and Power* (New York: Basic Books, 1989), 13.

2. Autoline Network, "The ART of Audi," YouTube video, 1:04:45, August 22, 2014, https://youtu.be/Y6ymjyPryRo.

3. Sharon Gaudin, "New Markets Push Strong Growth in Robotics Industry," *ComputerWorld*, February 26, 2016, http://www.computerworld .com/article/3038721/robotics/new-markets-push-strong-growth-in-robotics -industry.html.

4. Spencer Soper and Olivia Zaleski, "Inside Amazon's Battle to Break into the $800 Billion Grocery Market," Bloomberg, March 20, 2017, https:// www.bloomberg.com/news/features/2017-03-20/inside-amazon-s-battle-to -break-into-the-800-billion-grocery-market.

5. Izzie Lapowski, "Jeff Bezos Defends the Fire Phone's Flop and Amazon's Dismal Earnings," *Wired*, December 2, 2014, https://www.wired .com/2014/12/jeff-bezos-ignition-conference/.

6. Ben Fox Rubin, "Amazon's Store of the Future Is Delayed. Now What?" *CNET*, June 20, 2017, www.cnet.com/news/amazon-go-so-far-is-a -no-show-now-what/.

7. Steven Overly, "The Big Moral Dilemma Facing Self-Driving Cars," *Washington Post*, February 20, 2017, https://www.washingtonpost .com/news/innovations/wp/2017/02/20/the-big-moral-dilemma-facing-self -driving-cars/?utm_term=.e12ae9dedb61.

8. Matthew Hutson, "Why We Need to Learn to Trust Robots," *Boston Globe*, January 25, 2015, https://www.bostonglobe.com/ideas/2015/01/25 /why-need-learn-trust-robots/Nj6yQ5DSNsuTQlMcqnVQEI/story.html.

9. Aaron Timms, "Leda Braga: Machines Are the Future of Trading," *Institutional Investor,* July 15, 2015, http://www.institutionalinvestor.com /article/3471429/banking-and-capital-markets-trading-and-technology/leda -braga-machines-are-the-future-of-trading.html.

10. Accenture Research Survey, January 2017; and Lee Rainie and Janna Anderson, "Code-Dependent: Pros and Cons of the Algorithm Age," Pew Research, February 8, 2017, http://www.pewinternet.org/2017/02/08 /code-dependent-pros-and-cons-of-the-algorithm-age/.

11. Jane Wakefield, "Microsoft Chatbot Is Taught to Swear on Twitter," *BBC*, March 24, 2016, http://www.bbc.com/news/technology-35890188.

12. Craig Le Clair et al., "The Future of White-Collar Work: Sharing Your Cubicle with Robots," *Forrester*, June 22, 2016.

13. Madeline Clare Elish, "The Future of Designing Autonomous Systems Will Involve Ethnographers," *Ethnography Matters*, June 28, 2016,

https://ethnographymatters.net/blog/2016/06/28/the-future-of-designing
-autonomous-systems-will-involve-ethnographers/.

14. Madeleine Clare Elish, "Letting Autopilot Off the Hook," *Slate*,
June 16, 2016, www.slate.com/articles/technology/future_tense/2016/06
/why_do_blame_humans_when_automation_fails.html.

15. Berkeley J. Dietvorst et al, "Overcoming Algorithm Aversion: People
Will Use Imperfect Algorithms If They Can (Even Slightly) Modify Them,
https://poseidon01.ssrn.com/delivery.php?ID=93912406709202706700401412209507112202405505201500702907509708403011408111707100511701002504003002809903302910808507808411008505803204204707811610606811407209107200701706605311908412600106406609103011001509110801110508206809708811812601609909309602409&EXT=pdf.

16. Conversation with Bill Ruh, CEO for General Electric Digital,
April 11, 2017.

17. Ibid.

18. Accenture client work and Accenture Research case example
research findings (estimate)

19. Nicholas Fearn, "Ducati Corse Turns to IoT to Test MotoGP
Racing," *Internet of Business*, March 8, 2017, https://internetofbusiness
.com/ducati-corse-races-iot/.

20. Anthony Ha, "Salesforce Acquires Smart Calendar App Tempo, App
Will Shut Down on June 30," *Tech Crunch*, May 29, 2015, https://techcrunch
.com/2015/05/29/salesforce-acquires-tempo/.

21. "Nielsen Breakthrough Innovation Report, European Edition,"
Nielsen, December 2015, http://www.nielsen.com/content/dam
/nielsenglobal/eu/docs/pdf/Nielsen%20Breakthrough%20Innovation%20
Report%202015%20European%20Edition_digital_HU.pdf.

22. Mike Rogoway, "Facebook Plans 'Cold Storage' for Old Photos in
Prineville," *Oregonian*, February 20, 2013, http://www.oregonlive
.com/silicon-forest/index.ssf/2013/02/facebook_plans_cold_storage_fo.html.

23. "Illuminating Data," Texas Medical Center, August 24, 2014,
http://www.tmc.edu/news/2014/08/illuminating-data/.

24. George Wang, "Texas Medical Center and Ayasdi to Create a
World-Class Center for Complex Data Research and Innovation," Ayasdi,
November 13, 2013, https://www.ayasdi.com/company/news-and-events
/press/pr-texas-medical-center-and-ayasdi-to-create-a-world-class-center
-for-complex-data-research-and-innovation/.

25. Khari Johnson, "Google's Tensorflow Team Open-Sources Speech
Recognition Dataset for DIY AI," *VentureBeat*, August 24, 2017, https://

venturebeat.com/2017/08/24/googles-tensorflow-team-open-sources
-speech-recognition-dataset-for-diy-ai/.

26. Adam Liptak, "Sent to Prison by a Software Program's Secret
Algorithms," *New York Times*, May 1, 2017, https://www.nytimes.com
/2017/05/01/us/politics/sent-to-prison-by-a-software-programs-secret
-algorithms.html?_r=0.

27. Tim Lang, "Why Google's PAIR Initiative to Take Bias out of AI
Will Never Be Complete," *VentureBeat*, July 18, 2017, https://venturebeat
.com/2017/07/18/why-googles-pair-initiative-to-take-bias-out-of-ai-will
-never-be-complete/.

Chapter 8

1. GE Digital, "Minds + Machines: Meet the Digital Twin," YouTube
video, 14:18 minutes, November 18, 2016, https://www.youtube.com
/watch?v=2dCz3oL2rTw.

2. "Harnessing Revolution: Creating the Future Workforce," Accenture, https://www.accenture.com/gb-en/insight-future-workforce-today.

3. Marina Gorbis, "Human Plus Machine," The Future of Human
Machine Interaction, Institute for the Future, 2011, http://www.iftf.org
/uploads/media/Human_Plus_Machine_MG_sm.pdf.

4. Dan Ariely, James B. Duke, and William L. Lanier, "Disturbing
Trends in Physician Burnout and Satisfaction with Work-Life Balance,"
Mayo Clinic Proceedings 90, no. 12 (December 2015): 1593–1596.

5. Wes Venteicher, "UPMC Turns to Artificial Intelligence to Ease
Doctor Burnout," *TribLive*, February 16, 2017, http://triblive.com/news
/healthnow/11955589-74/burnout-doctors-microsoft.

6. Bob Rogers, "Making Healthcare More Human with Artificial Intelligence," *IT Peer Network at Intel*, February 17, 2017, https://itpeernetwork
.intel.com/making-healthcare-human-artificial-intelligence/.

7. Conner Dial, "Audi Makes Self-Driving Cars Seem Normal By Putting a T-Rex at the Wheel," *PSFK*, September 16, 2016, https://www.psfk
.com/2016/09/audi-t-rex-ad-campaign-makes-self-driving-vehicles-seem
-normal.html.

8. "AI Summit New York," *AI Business*, 2016, http://aibusiness.org/tag
/ai-summit-new-york/.

9. Ibid.

10. Murray Shanahan, "The Frame Problem," Stanford, February 23,
2004, https://plato.stanford.edu/entries/frame-problem/.

11. Manoj Sahi, "Sensabot Is the First Inspection Robot Approved for
Use by Oil and Gas Companies," *Tractica*, October 18, 2016, https://www

.tractica.com/robotics/sensabot-is-the-first-inspection-robot-approved-for
-use-by-oil-and-gas-companies/.

12. Author interview with Steve Schnur, December 7, 2016.

13. Author interview with Bill Ruh, April 11, 2017.

14. Shivon Zilis, "Machine Intelligence Will Let Us All Work Like
CEOs," *Harvard Business Review*, June 13, 2013, https://hbr.org/2016/06
/machine-intelligence-will-let-us-all-work-like-ceos.

15. Julie Bort, "How Salesforce CEO Marc Benioff Uses Artificial
Intelligence to End Internal Politics at Meetings," *Business Insider*, May 18,
2017, www.businessinsider.com/benioff-uses-ai-to-end-politics-at-staff
-meetings-2017-5.

16. "Surgeons Use Robot to Operate Inside Eye in World's First," *The
Guardian*, September 9, 2016, https://www.theguardian.com/technology
/2016/sep/10/robot-eye-operation-world-first-oxford-john-radcliffe.

17. Will Knight, "How a Human-Machine Mind-Meld Could Make
Robots Smarter," *MIT Technology Review*, March 2, 2017, https://www
.technologyreview.com/s/603745/how-a-human-machine-mind-meld-could
-make-robots-smarter/.

18. Janet Vertesi, "What Robots in Space Teach Us about Teamwork: A Deep Dive into NASA," *Ethnography Matters*, July 7, 2016, http://
ethnographymatters.net/blog/2016/07/07/what-robots-in-space-teach-us-
about-teamwork/.

19. Pierre Nanterme and Paul Daugherty, "Technology for People:
The Era of Intelligent Enterprise," Technology Vision 2017, https://www
.accenture.com/t00010101T000000__w__/at-de/_acnmedia/Accenture
/next-gen-4/tech-vision-2017/pdf/Accenture-TV17-Full.pdf.

20. Justin Bariso, "Microsoft's CEO Just Gave Some Brilliant Career
Advice. Here It Is in 1 Sentence," *Inc.com*, April 24, 2017, https://www.inc
.com/justin-bariso/microsofts-ceo-just-gave-some-brilliant-career-advice
-here-it-is-in-one-sentence.html.

21. Sara Castellanos, "Capital One Adds 'Muscle' to Machine Learning
Effort," *Wall Street Journal*, March 2, 2017, https://blogs.wsj.com
/cio/2017/03/02/capital-one-adds-muscle-to-machine-learning-effort/.

22. Darryl K. Taft, "Capital One Taps Open-Source, Cloud, Big Data for
Advantage in Banking," *eWEEK*, June 13, 2016, http://www.eweek.com/cloud
/capital-one-taps-open-source-cloud-big-data-for-advantage-in-banking.

23. Gil Press, "3 Dimensions of Digital Transformation at Capital One
Financial Services," *Forbes*, June 25, 2015, https://www.forbes.com/sites
/gilpress/2015/06/25/3-dimensions-of-digital-transformation-at-capital
-one-financial-services/#61620c4478c4.

24. Andy Clark, *Supersizing the Mind: Embodiment, Action, and Cognitive Extension* (New York: Oxford University Press, 2008).

Conclusion

1. Seth G. Benzell, Laurence J. Kotlikoff, Guillermo LaGarda, Jeffrey D. Sachs, "Robots Are Us: Some Economics of Human Replacement," NBER Working Paper No. 20941, Issued in February 2015

2. Anna Louie Sussman, "As Skill Requirements Increase, More Manufacturing Jobs Go Unfilled," *The Wall Street Journal*, September 1, 2016, https://www.wsj.com/articles/as-skill-requirements-increase-more-manufacturing-jobs-go-unfilled-1472733676

3. Analysis of IMF and Indeed.com data by George Washington University economist Tara Sinclair, http://offers.indeed.com/rs/699-SXJ-715/images/Indeed%20Hiring%20Lab%20- %20Labor%20Market%20Outlook%202016.pdf.

4. 2017 Accenture Research analysis, https://www.accenture.com/us-en/_ acnmedia/A2F06B52B774493BBBA35EA27BCDFCE7.pdf. See also, World Economic Forum, *Future of Jobs Report*, http://reports.weforum.org/future-of-jobs-2016/.

5. Kristin Majcher, "The Hunt for Qualified Workers," *MIT Technology Review*, September 16, 2014, https://www.technologyreview.com/s/530701/the-hunt-for-qualified-workers/.

6. "Artificial Intelligence, Automation, and the Economy," The White House, December 20, 2016, https://www.whitehouse.gov/sites/whitehouse.gov/files/images/EMBARGOED%20AI%20Economy%20Report.pdf.

7. Datainnovation.org, https://www.datainnovation.org/2017/08/how-governments-arepreparing-for-artificial-intelligence/.

8. The State Council of the People's Republic of China, http://english.gov.cn/policies/latest_releases/2017/07/20/content_281475742458322.htm.

INDEX

ACKNOWLEDGMENTS

The development of *Human + Machine* has been a fascinating journey, born over a cup coffee in Boston's Copley Plaza almost two years ago, and influenced by thousands of experiences along the way—conversations with executives, entrepreneurs, workers, AI experts, technologists, economists, social scientists, policymakers, futurists, venture capitalists, educators, students, among others. We are indebted to the multitude of people from all corners of the world who have spent many hours with us discussing, shaping, and of course debating key topics in the book.

We would like to thank our many colleagues who helped shape our vision for *Human + Machine*, as well as the incredible team of smart people (often using smart machines) who contributed to this book.

An amazing researcher and collaborator, Kate Greene was in the trenches of AI R&D with us from early on. We are incredibly grateful for Kate's multidisciplinary mind and her dedication to this project throughout. Likewise, David Lavieri and Prashant Shukla worked with us week in, week out to solidify the research foundations of *Human + Machine*'s core ideas, including the "missing middle."

Francis Hintermann and his Accenture Research team provided world-class expertise and unfailing support for the project. Paul Nunes was a very early champion of the book and a reviewer at key stages in its development, offering incisive and practical comments. Special thanks to Allan Alter, who played a crucial role early in the book's development by contributing to the design of our survey and case research on fair, safe, and responsible AI. Many other researchers provided relevant findings and insights that enriched our thinking, including Mark Purdy, Ladan Davarzani, Athena Peppes, Philippe Roussiere, Svenja Falk, Raghav Narsalay, Madhu Vazirani, Sybille Berjoan, Mamta Kapur, Renee Byrnes, Tomas Castagnino, Caroline Liu, Lauren Finkelstein, Andrew Cavanaugh, and Nick Yennaco.

We owe a special debt to the many visionaries and pioneers who have blazed AI trails and whose work has inspired and informed us, including Herbert Simon, John McCarthy, Marvin Minsky, Arthur Samuel, Edward Feigenbaum, Joseph Weizenbaum, Geoffrey Hinton, Hans Moravec, Peter Norvig, Douglas Hofstadter, Ray Kurzweil, Rodney Brooks, Yann LeCun, and Andrew Ng, among many others. And huge gratitude to our colleagues who provided insights and inspiration, including Nicola Morini Bianzino, Mike Sutcliff, Ellyn Shook, Marc Carrel-Billiard, Narendra Mulani, Dan Elron, Frank Meerkamp, Adam Burden, Mark McDonald, Cyrille Bataller, Sanjeev Vohra, Rumman Chowdhury, Lisa Neuberger-Fernandez, Dadong Wan, Sanjay Podder, and Michael Biltz. They are on the leading edge of AI, charting the course and truly "reimagining" business.

Throughout this journey, we were advised by a diverse group of publishing and marketing pros who helped us fine-tune our message. Early on, Giles Anderson at the Anderson Literary Agency helped shape our proposal and find the right press and platform for it. Jeff Kehoe, Kenzie Travers, and Dave Lievens at HBR Press were our literary field guides, providing strong support from the start, and wisdom and guidance as we navigated through revisions.

The book—and our readers—are beneficiaries of fantastic editorial and marketing expertise, starting with Roxanne Taylor, Jeff Francis, Shari Wenker, Elise Cornille, Anuneha Mewawalla, Peter Soh, Ed Maney, Gwen Harrigan, Carolyn Monaco, Jill Totenberg, and Clare Huisamen, who all helped us think carefully about how to communicate and connect the *Human + Machine* themes to our audience. Dave Light offered useful guidance on structure and chapter flow early in the book's development and ensured the right editorial resources were in place throughout. On that note, we'd like to thank Alden Hayashi. A brilliant editorial mind and a wonderful person to work with, Alden played a vital role in helping shape and refine the manuscript.

We extend special thanks to Pierre Nanterme, Accenture's CEO, for supporting us in writing the book, and moreover, for his vision and leadership in steering Accenture on a truly human + machine course. And we'd like to recognize Omar Abbosh, Accenture's Chief Strategy Officer and head of Accenture Research, who has been with us all the way, providing sponsorship and insights.

Our gratitude also extends to the many pioneering clients who have entrusted Accenture to be their guide as they apply AI to 'reimagine' their business and approach to work. We've had the unique privilege not only to research the ideas in this book, but also to apply concepts and observe the results from these true pioneers in the age of AI.

And finally, on a more personal note . . .

Paul: A heartfelt thanks to my wife, Beth, whose passion and commitment to human potential always inspires me and led to the core premise of the book. Emma, Jesse, Johnny, and Lucy provided the balance I needed—tolerating my book work on evenings, weekends, and vacations but also dragging me away when necessary and always making me laugh. And I must also acknowledge my father, whose love for people and delight in tinkering with technology set me on this course.

Jim: I'd like to thank my family for their amazing support. As deadlines loomed, Susan and Brooke Wilson always managed to put a smile on my face by making funny-sounding 1950s sci-fi robot voices. Benjamin Wilson's passion for reading works at the frontiers of the human imagination has been an ongoing inspiration. I'd also like to acknowledge my parents, Betsy and Jim, for their love and encouragement.

ABOUT THE AUTHORS

PAUL DAUGHERTY and **H. JAMES (JIM) WILSON**, senior executives at Accenture, have long collaborated to research and document the impact that technology is having on business and society. They have studied the evolution of artificial intelligence over the last three decades.

More recently, as AI burst onto the public stage and into headlines and trending topics, Daugherty and Wilson realized that the debates of the day were very subjective, often based on opinion, and that there was no research or data on *how* AI will drive change and *what* changes are needed today and in the future. More significantly, there was little objective guidance for those who need to make important decisions *today* on how to apply AI to business, government, and education. And with that, the research program at the heart of *Human + Machine* was born.

With Daugherty's experience helping organizations make major shifts driven by technology and Wilson's technology strategy and research expertise, they decided to shed light on what the "Age of AI" entails, and together they wrote *Human + Machine: Reimagining Work in the Age of AI.*

PAUL DAUGHERTY is Accenture's Chief Technology and Innovation Officer. Over his career, he has worked with thousands of business and government leaders around the globe, helping them apply technology to transform their organizations. He has also been instrumental in evolving Accenture's business to respond to the exponential changes in technology.

Daugherty oversees Accenture's technology strategy and innovation architecture, and he leads Accenture's research and development, ventures, advanced technology, and ecosystem groups. He recently founded Accenture's artificial intelligence business and has led Accenture's research into artificial intelligence over many years.

Daugherty studied computer engineering at the University of Michigan in the early 1980s, and on a whim took a course with Douglas Hofstadter on cognitive science and psychology. He was hooked, and this led to a career-long pursuit of AI.

A frequent speaker and writer on industry and technology issues, Daugherty has been featured in a variety of media outlets, including the *Financial Times, MIT Sloan Management Review, Forbes, Fast Company, USA Today, Fortune, Harvard Business Review*, Cheddar financial news network, Bloomberg Television, and CNBC. He was recently named as one of *Computerworld*'s Premier 100 Technology Leaders for 2017 for his extraordinary technology leadership.

Daugherty is a passionate advocate for equal opportunity and access to technology and computer science. He serves on the board of directors of Girls Who Code and is a strong advocate and sponsor of Code.org. He was also recognized with an Institute for Women's Leadership award, honoring business leaders who have supported diversity in the workplace and the advancement of women.

In addition, Daugherty serves as chairman of the board of Avanade and is on the board of trustees of the Computer History Museum. He is a member of the World Economic Forum Global Future Council on the Future of Artificial Intelligence and Robotics, and he is on the advisory board for Computer Science and Engineering at the University of Michigan.

Daugherty lives in Maplewood, New Jersey, with his wife, Beth. He has four children, Emma, Jesse, Johnny, and Lucy, who are all charting their own courses for the human + machine future.

H. JAMES (JIM) WILSON leads Accenture's Information Technology and Business Research. He has dedicated his career to research and innovation, having led programs at Babson Executive and Enterprise Education, Bain & Company, and several businessthink tanks. Wilson is a coauthor of *The New Entrepreneurial Leader*, which pioneered a new approach—entrepreneurial leadership—developed by him and a team of experts at Babson College.

A long-time contributor to *Harvard Business Review*, *MIT Sloan Management Review*, and the *Wall Street Journal*, Wilson has written extensively on how smart machines can enhance worker performance, including some of the first *HBR* articles on personal analytics, social IT, wearables, and natural user interfaces.

Wilson has worked with governments, policy makers, and university and business leaders in applying these technologies to empower and augment people—from NASA to the NFL Players Association.

An avid triathlete, Wilson enjoys teaching friends and family his geeky techniques for boosting health and fitness using bike power meters, heart rate monitors, and GPS distance and pace trackers. He lives in San Francisco with his wife, Susan, and two children, Ben and Brooke.